SAVING AMERICA

J. Hartz

2010

SAVING AMERICA

★★★★★★★★★★★★★★★★★★★★★★

Common Sense Solutions
to Washington Nonsense

BY JIM H. HOUTZ

Published by Howard Claire, LLC
15802 N. 71st Street, Unit 651
Scottsdale, Arizona 85254
480-275-5450
www.jimhhoutz.com

Edited by Barbara Toombs, Phoenix, Arizona
Cover Design by Robert Renteria, Phoenix, Arizona
Produced by Cloud Nine Press, LLC, Scottsdale, Arizona

Publisher's Cataloguing-in-Publication Data (Provided by Quality Books, Inc.)
Houtz, Jim H.
Saving America: common sense solutions to Washington
nonsense / by Jim H. Houtz.
p. cm.
Includes bibliographical references and index.
ISBN–13: 978–0–9826371–0–4
ISBN–10: 0–9826371–0–1

1. United States—Politics and government—2009–
2. Washington (D.C.)—Politics and government. I. Title.

E907.H68 2010   973.932
                                                QBI10-600025

Dedication

This book is dedicated to the men and women who have served our country in the United States Armed Forces. To all of them, we cannot show our appreciation enough. I try to say, "Thanks for serving" whenever I see a service person in uniform, and it's not nearly often enough. So allow me to say it here, too. Thanks for doing what is required to save our way of life and all of our tremendous freedoms.

There are an unlimited number of stories about war experiences out there. The most recent one I heard was also the most emotional for me. While I was waiting for an elevator at the Mayo Clinic in Scottsdale, Arizona, a gentleman in his early eighties stood next to me. He, too, was waiting for an elevator. I looked over and on his head was a baseball cap that said "Iwo Jima." Iwo Jima is an island in the Pacific where several thousand Marines were killed in one of the most devastating battles of World War II. I asked him, "Were you there?"

He said, "Yes I was," and proceeded to tell me the following story. "My twin brother and I were in the same platoon that went ashore; he was killed the first day. When it was time for our platoon of ninety-six soldiers to the leave the island, I was the only one who made it off Iwo Jima." He then said, "It has been over fifty years since it happened, and I still get choked up whenever I talk about it."

We both stood in the elevator waiting area with tears in our eyes. The only thing I could think to say was, "Thanks for serving." He nodded; the up and down elevators came at the same time, and we went our separate ways. I have thought about this hero (whose name I do not know), his twin brother, and the other soldiers in his platoon of ninety-six numerous times. How terrifying their experiences and last moments must have been. Somehow, "Thanks for serving" doesn't seem like enough.

We owe all current and past service personnel a debt of gratitude that can only be paid by making sure we (you and I) do everything possible to maintain the strength and freedom of our country. I am hopeful this book will be one single step in that direction. Like simply saying thank you, it is still not enough … but it's a start.

Acknowledgments

The inspiration for this book came from the Tea Parties and the people who are part of them. Their commitment to a cause and the concern they demonstrate for America is obvious in the number of people who show up to express their concern about the direction the White House and Congress are taking our country. We want our freedom back.

I have never viewed the Tea Party movement as something organized by Republicans, Democrats, or Independents, but rather as a groundswell, a grassroots movement by the citizens of America, within the communities of America. These meetings were initially inspired by the media and disparaged by House and Senate leaders, but people kept coming and the Tea Parties became larger and larger.

When history is written, I believe the 2009 and 2010 Tea Parties will be recognized as a pivotal action that changed the direction of America. Special thanks should go to those Americans who generously gave their time to get involved and have their opinions heard.

Although I wrote the chapters on health care and entrepreneurship primarily from my almost forty years' experience in those two fields, I did not write this book alone. The chapters have been supported by a significant amount of research and analysis.

I would like to thank:
- Kathy Heasley, my co-writer
- Pam Swartz, my book shepherd
- Craig Morgan, for support on three chapters
- Ben Aguilera, for assistance and advice on the immigration chapter
- Mike Heasley, my project manager

It took several months to draft the first manuscript and another two months of rewrites, but throughout it all, my wife Joyce was very supportive (and frequently the first reader).

Once again, to all the Tea Party participants, you are doing a great job. I believe your actions will change the direction of America. Keep doing it!

Table of Contents

The Freedom Creed
by Jim H. Houtz 09-09-09

Freedom has a cost: eternal vigilance.

We believe... Today, we are in a struggle with our government, a government that appears non-responsive and is destroying small business.

We admit... All parties have exceeded reasonable government spending levels. Neither Republicans, Democrats, nor Independents can claim they are immune, because they are not.

We cast our vote... So our elected officials would represent us, but it is clear our Congress represents primarily itself, and considers us all a nuisance, except on Election Day.

We have experienced... Severe economic strife, and already the private sector has lost several industries: home lending, banking, automotive, energy... with more on the way. Will communications and aviation be next?

We wonder... Why our government has over thirty czars. They are not approved or directed by Congress, and appear to have powers unknown to the American people.

We ask... Is it our government's intent to control all industries and "reform" each one as they see fit, through legislation? We will resist. Individually, we can be broken. United, no one can break us.

We are committed... To first, protect our industries, and then help others protect theirs, by alerting each other to the impending changes.

We will keep our method simple... It's time to reignite the entrepreneurs of America. They are the innovators, the risk takers, our future. They will know what to do.

Our day of reckoning is here. Stand now for freedom.

WE CAN MAKE A DIFFERENCE

The Tea Party participants
Have awakened our spirit.
It will demand all our participation
To control government spending.

Saving America is one man's hope to bring our country together. We have no greater obligation than to preserve this great land—this shining city on a hill—for our children, our grandchildren, and all of our descendants.

America has become more than a country, more than a place governed by the rule of law, more than the land of opportunity. It has been, and should continue to be, a place of hope for the entire world.

As you read this book, you may wonder if I am a Republican, Democrat, or Independent; a Conservative or a Liberal; a neo-conservative or an ultra-liberal. Actually, I am none of these and yet I am some of each, but most importantly I am an American. And very proud of it.

I am also a lifelong entrepreneur, and as a young man I was told, "You think differently than most of us." That statement used to really make me mad, because I didn't *want* to be different. However, as I became older I realized the assessment was accurate and the statement was correct. I *do* think differently than most people. I think like the thousands of entrepreneurs who have helped put America together. When confronted with a problem, we try to figure out the core issue, rather than address the several, or several dozen, or several hundred symptoms.

Entrepreneurs know that when we solve the core problem or issue, all the other troublesome symptoms disappear. This book defines eight major areas that have a significant impact on the future of our country. All of them generate a considerable number of symptoms that parade as problems.

These eight major issues—energy, health care, entrepreneurship, immigration, Congress, the military, education, and the economy—represent most of what we Americans deal with on a daily basis. We do not deal with terrorism in this book, but address it indirectly with emphasis on immigration and the military.

I have lived through the leadership of thirteen presidents to date. I remember President Roosevelt only vaguely. From Truman on, I do not believe the level of disconnect between the American public and its elected officials in the White House and Congress has ever been as great as it is today. The Tea Parties have been an incredible, positive series of citizen meetings, where the voters have expressed their outrage in a civilized and peaceful manner. I believe Tea Party participants have come from all parties—Republican, Democrat, and Independents.

The original issue that ignited the citizens' uprising was health care. As the Tea Party movement began to gain intensity, the Democrats in control of Congress didn't listen, but instead chose to increase spending and began buying (bribing) health care votes. They may as well have pumped gasoline on a raging fire.

I believe the Tea Parties will long be remembered as positive, direction-changing events for America. This book is about the issues the Tea Parties will eventually need to address. Most of the solutions are simple in concept yet very difficult in execution. They are not, however, beyond the capability of the American people.

In this book's dedication, I introduced you to an elderly gentleman who is a member of our "Greatest Generation." We owe our freedom to him, to his twin brother, and to the other ninety-four members of his platoon still at Iwo Jima. We owe it to *all* the American service people who gave (and still give) bravely and tirelessly, preserving freedom throughout the world. It's especially dedicated to those who did not come back. In honor of them, it's time to address these issues, solve the core problems, and get it right.

When we are finished correcting our current skirmishes between the people, the White House, and Congress, I think we will look back and say, "Compared to what our military personnel have gone through over the years, this wasn't so tough."

Good luck with the book. Enjoy reading it—and then let's get to work to correct the government.

—Jim H. Houtz
An American Entrepreneur

CURRENT STATUS

CHAPTER 1

★★★★★★★★★★★★★★★★★★★★★★★★

OVERVIEW OF ISSUES

America the great,
America the beautiful
Requires our help
To preserve our future.

Right now...

Take a picture of America right now. What do you see? What I see is that right now, the political climate is having a dramatic impact on the effectiveness of Congress and the White House. Major problems in America that appear to have simple solutions have become complicated. Particularly when every member of Congress is determined to have his or her pet issue, state, or district's special interest included in legislation, the way he or she wants it, or no deal. This kind of "my way or the highway" behavior isn't new on Capitol Hill. It's been going on for decades. But just because it is "business as usual" doesn't mean we can afford to *keep* it that way. If we are going to save America, something has to change ... right now.

The Current Political Climate in Congress

All representatives and senators are elected to represent their districts or their states, and the citizens who reside there. They also are expected to protect the interests of America. Yet it appears their primary interest is to represent their own personal interests—as well as the interests of their political party. Their behaviors, rather than being about furthering the nation and people living within its borders, have been about pandering to special interest groups.

House and Senate leaders control the purse strings for earmarks and "special considerations," which outside the Beltway are known as bribes. The practice of special interest groups buying votes has enraged the American population. Many House and Senate leaders will probably say they are not involved, or that it is not as it seems. Maybe so. We have strange criminal laws in America. Here in this country, if you know of a crime and do nothing to stop it or if you fail to report it, you are just as guilty as the actual participants. Maybe that law doesn't apply in the District of Columbia.

I know old-fashioned common sense and morality might not be of interest to the elitists in Congress, but hopefully those elitists will not be there for long.

The press and the pundits aren't helping matters any. They like to divide people into groups. The political groups or audiences are neo-conservatives, conservatives, independents, liberals, and ultra-liberals. I believe Congress is comprised of a much higher percentage of neo-conservatives and ultra-liberals than we have in America's general populace. I think we need a break from the neo-conservatives and ultra-liberals in Congress. Let's let the moderates have a shot at addressing the issues in this book. Unfortunately, we have ultra-liberals in charge of the House, Senate, and White House. In the fall of 2010 we have a chance to change two of the three, and impact the direction of the White House.

The Current Political Climate in the White House

Here in the first quarter of 2010 things are a little tense. If health care reform had been approached as a true bipartisan effort, the result might have been a plan the public would have accepted. It is somewhat irrelevant whether the health care bill passes or not, because the American people will not accept it. If passed, it will be modified or rescinded. The proposed Cap and Trade bill to control greenhouse gas emissions is recognized as a joke, and will never pass the Senate. The current socialist agenda is under attack; the public has become aware of what "income distribution" really means and we do not like it.

Our current president could take a couple of lessons in leadership. You never make much headway by bashing your team in public. So far, a brief list of people the president has degraded publicly include fat-cat bankers, business people who use private aviation, Wall Street executives, physicians, insurance companies, Fox News, oil companies, greedy business people, and just about everyone else who has figured out how to make a profit. (Would someone please tell the president that taxes come from profits?)

To be an effective leader, one of the first things you learn is: praise in public, critique in private. The president is in charge of the economy, and even though he may not like it, the business community is part of his team. It may be too late, but he should start inspiring and using that community.

In this book, I cover the eight major issues we face right now as a nation. Here is a quick rundown:

1. **Saving Our Energy Supply**
    All the subjects I am addressing are important; however, I address energy first, because it is the one most critical to our future. We need a comprehensive energy policy that recognizes our continued emphasis on fossil fuels will lead to disastrous results. The world is rapidly depleting its supply of oil, and with China and India predicted to significantly increase their use of oil, we need to find other sources of energy now. This is not something you can do overnight; it will take several years to develop these sources.

2. **Saving Health Care**
    I have spent almost forty years as an entrepreneur in health care. I know—I am old, but I am still doing it! Our health care system is outstanding; however, like anything else, it can be improved.

We need health care reform that will *help* the system, not destroy it. Read the chapter on health care and compare it to what Congress puts before us, then draw your own conclusions.

3. Saving Entrepreneurship

Where is John Galt, the mythical entrepreneur in Ayn Rand's book *Atlas Shrugged*, when you need him? He is probably off building a new power supply. I do not think anyone in the White House has a clue about how to build an economy or create new jobs. According to a study reviewed in *Investor's Business Daily*, the current White House staff has the lowest number of people with business experience of any administration in the last 100 years. This chapter on entrepreneurship outlines a simple plan that would get people back to work and stave off another financial crisis.

4. Saving Immigration

Every president has to deal with immigration. To date, none of them have addressed the key issue, which is to have control of our borders. We can pass into law any kind of immigration policy imaginable, but until we control our borders we will not have control of immigration. With one exception, the issues on immigration and the solutions are fairly clear and easy to solve. The one issue that does *not* have a clear solution is what to do about the illegal immigrants who are already in the country. But not to disappoint, I pose a solution to that, too.

5. Saving Congress

This chapter really should be called "Saving Congress from Itself." Congress, especially the Senate, used to be one of the most respected entities in the country. That was before earmarks, payoffs, lobbyist fees, and a host of other income-generating fees members of Congress enjoy. I agree: their votes are not for sale—

unless, of course, it's for a really big number. Please! Before I vote for anyone, I want to know his or her position on earmarks and selling of votes, as well as his or her representation priority: America, the citizens, the party, or self. We need people from both parties who are fiscally responsible, dedicated to our national defense, have the ability to help build the economy, and have a strong dose of common sense.

6. Saving the Military

I love our military. I have more respect for the military than for any other organization in the world. Any time I hear some dumb member of Congress talk about cutting back our military, I really get ticked! Without the military, our country would never have generated the standard of living we have, and very possibly would not exist. Our volunteer force needs to remain just that: volunteer. To continue to attract volunteers, we need to make sure we take care of all of our veterans in terms of health care and employment when they complete their service. Make sure whenever you encounter a military person, active or retired, that you thank them for their service. That on its own is not enough, but it is a start.

7. Saving Education

Math, science, history, and English: teaching these core courses has been and always will be our main emphasis. Why is there so much criticism regarding education? I cover some startling statistics that mirror the problem we face as a nation. More money won't help. There's enough money; it's just not being allocated the right way. And there's enough blame to go around. Unions, policymakers, administrators, teachers, students, parents—you name it. I make the case and pose a plan to fix the problems we face in our schools. But I can't fix the problem within our homes. At the risk of sounding preachy or coach-like, hear me out. I *am* a coach, not for high school or college teams, but for grade school boys' basketball. Every year I discuss "referees" with them. The discussion is short, and goes like this: "No matter what happens, you only have two things you can say to a ref. They are: 'Yes, Sir' and 'No Sir.' No exceptions!" I do not believe our team has had any technical fouls in seven years. The teams we have played, on the other hand, have had several. Having a "referee" discussion with your son or daughter might help. Discipline is a prerequisite for *any* successful education system.

8. Saving the Economy

Several projections say we are going to have a recovery without any significant increase in jobs. If we leave it up to the White House and Congress that's probably what we *will* have. Well, that is not good enough. We need some stability in Washington, D.C. But in addition to that, the growth must come from us—the citizens of this country, its business people, and the entrepreneurs. Earlier in this chapter I asked, "Where is John Galt?" Well, he is *us*, and it is up to us to get this economy going. I am trying to step up; we need you to do the same.

Echoes From the Past

When President Reagan came into office, he wanted to cut taxes and build the military. Thomas "Tip" O'Neill was Speaker of the House, and he wanted several domestic programs instead. They belonged to different parties, but they worked together as Americans and developed a compromise; each was able to do what he wanted with the help of the other. What do you suppose would have happened in 2009 if Reagan and O'Neill were in office? My guess is we would have a health care reform act that the public loved and would be very close to what I have recommended. They also would have done it without any payoffs or special considerations.

I wonder if members of Congress ever visit Arlington National Cemetery, the Vietnam Veterans Memorial, or the Soldiers' National Cemetery at Gettysburg. They should do so, and ask themselves what those military souls were serving and fighting for. Were the soldiers thinking about themselves, how much money they could make, or the special benefits they could scam? Or were they thinking about not letting their fellow soldiers down and protecting the country? I believe a major reason for the citizens' outrage with the way things are right now has to do with the fact that members of Congress have put their own interests ahead of the citizens' interests.

The current occupants of the White House are experiencing the same outrage the citizens displayed for Richard Nixon and Bill Clinton. Nixon had a problem with Watergate, and Clinton had some personal problems. The outrage against both peaked when the public realized they had been duped. Barack Obama is rapidly approaching the same level of outrage for almost exactly the same reason: a lack of trust.

Right now, we need change. Right now, we need some leadership. And right now, we need some action. *Saving America* is your handbook.

CORRECTIVE STEPS

★★★★★★★★★★★★★★★★★★★★★★★★

★★★★★★★★★★★★★★★★★★★★★★★★★

CHAPTER 2

SAVING OUR ENERGY SUPPLY

We have built our nation
With low-cost energy.
To continue that growth,
We need alternative sources.

Lately, it doesn't matter which election it is, whether we're choosing a president or senators or representatives, energy is an issue of debate. Of course the debate isn't about the obvious fact that we *need* energy to maintain our society and lifestyle, the debate is always about how we *acquire* that energy to meet the ever-growing world demand. In the 2008 election, we had John McCain shouting, "Drill, baby, drill," in his best rally-cry voice. And we had Barack Obama emphatically stating, "We must attain energy independence." In elections going forward, until we actually do more than *talk* about energy and actually *do* something about it, be prepared for the same two slogans that we have heard in just about every national election since the OPEC Oil Embargo of 1973 and, I might add, every time gas prices reach the point of pain for the average American. The slogans might be worded a little differently in each election, but stay tuned; you'll hear them when it is time to cast your vote or pay up at the pump.

Not only are we shallow and easily distracted by everything from job losses to Michael Jackson's coroner's report to whatever sports play-off seems to be going on at the moment, but our elected officials are shallow and easily distracted, too. Worst of all, they try to distract us during elections with the slogans they think their constituents want to hear. I don't fault the American people for being shallow and easily distracted. Most people are fed up and think the whole government is hopeless. May as well root for the Saints or the Sox or the Suns and wait for the latest celebrity death toxicology report. But I do fault our elected officials for being shallow and easily distracted. And I fault them for one other thing: trying to fool us into believing that they are actually trying to solve the energy problem with their bogus slogans.

Why all the fuss over a few catchy lines? Because words alone cannot and *do not* address our primary energy issues. They are merely tactics, and, as any business person knows, tactics without a strategy behind them are doomed to failure. You see, we don't need a few lines that make the people on one side of the aisle or the other cheer or boo. What we need is a comprehensive energy policy that addresses the major energy issues facing this country and the rest of the world. No matter how you slice it, the primary issue facing us all is singularly—and oh so obviously—the world's dependence on fossil fuels.

If I have to get into the slogan business to get people's attention, here's mine: "We must attain independence from fossil fuels." This chapter will convince you—I'm sure of it. My hope is that the validity of my argument will encourage you to do more than nod your head. I hope it causes you to take action to ensure that our children and our children's children aren't in the same mess we're in right now. Oh, yes, but of course they won't be, because by that time, the oil that's left will be too costly to extract. Our heirs will be sitting in the dark twiddling their thumbs. The future sounds lovely, doesn't it?

In this chapter, I'll talk about the concept known as Peak Oil, and I'll identify the issues we should be discussing and solving. As you are already beginning to see as you read this book, I take an entrepreneurial approach to all tough problems. I *am* an entrepreneur and, in truth, it's the entrepreneurs—not government officials—who have historically tackled and solved every major problem known to man. Yes, from the time our cave-dwelling ancestors decided they wanted a hot meal all the way to figuring out how we're going to use DNA to cure cancer, entrepreneurs have been in the forefront. The entrepreneurial approach *works*, and it's time we took this path. We can no longer wait for people who are beholden to lobbyists and special interest groups to sit around a table and talk, talk, talk. It's time for strategy. It's time for action.

You'll find my entrepreneurial approach first seeks to identify the most critical issues, and then poses a variety of solutions designed to deliver maximum benefit for the effort. Right now, we're seeing effort without any benefit at all. This has to stop. No one looks good in a parka—and heating in the winter and air conditioning in the summer are going to be tough to give up. C'mon, entrepreneurs, we need you now! This is your call to arms!

I have complete respect for entrepreneurs, because they are an amazing bunch. One of the things I respect the most about them is their tendency to ignore symptoms and instead go right to the source issue and solve it. That's how you make the symptoms disappear for good. Think of it this way: When the National Highway Safety Administration started reporting high rates of infant injury and death in traffic accidents, entrepreneurs didn't approach the problem by manufacturing more splints, bandages, and caskets. They addressed it by inventing increasingly safer car seats for babies. In the process they have saved countless lives, changed our behaviors, created a multi-billion dollar industry, and spawned thousands of jobs. That's what entrepreneurs do.

I realize this is very obvious to anyone who is, or has worked with or for, an entrepreneur. But if you haven't, this shift in thinking may be new to you. It certainly must be new thinking to our friends in Congress, because in the time they have been working for us, they have been more interested in buying bandages and spending as much of our money (yours and mine) as quickly as they possibly can. If only they would put the checkbook away and think strategically just this once, we might have an energy policy that actually works and that (can you imagine this?) inspires our country and everyone who lives within its borders to greatness.

You may read this chapter and conclude that I am a Democrat. Some of you will read it and conclude that I am a Republican. Some of my positions will seem to come from one or the other of these party playbooks. For the sake of this chapter and this book, let's drop the labels. Labeling, then taking sides, is the root of many problems in this country. Our energy challenge is not the Super Bowl. There's no basket of chips or tub of onion dip to accompany the discussion of what we should do and how to do it. One team doesn't have to win at the expense of the other. In case we forgot, we all have lungs that need air, and we all have lives that require we get from Point A to Point B at least a few times a week. Let's not make energy a competition or a battle of wills. Let's make it our generation's mission to solve.

So, if you must know, I consider myself a moderate, and this chapter, along with all the others, is written from the viewpoint of an American who deeply loves his country, but is disappointed in its lack of direction and focus. My words and intensity in this chapter come from this place, and my years of experience tell me our inaction is compromising our national stability and our personal freedom. If you believe that we can continue along the same path we are on and enjoy our prized American way of life, then you need to read this chapter more than most. If, on the other hand, you know that "something's gotta give," as they say, then read this chapter and see it as I do—as the most important action plan of our lives.

What Is Peak Oil? Why Does It Matter?

Any discussion of energy can't really be a discussion at all without covering the concept of Peak Oil. As the name implies, Peak Oil is that point in time when the maximum amount of global petroleum extraction reaches its peak. Once Peak Oil is attained, the result is terminal decline. Terminal decline means that, unlike other production ups and downs, there are no more ups. Oil production will be in a steady downward spiral. There are people who feel that unless we do something—and do something quickly—terminal decline will be the end of the world as we know it. Others feel that there will be enough oil to last us forever. My views fall somewhere in between. But make no mistake. In my opinion, releasing our self-imposed fossil fuel stranglehold is dire. If we don't fix this, nothing else in this book will really matter.

You might be wondering how we gauge both the amount of oil we have and the amount of oil we have left. It's not an exact science, but there are some very educated and experienced professionals inside and outside the petroleum industry who measure production and estimate future production day in and day out for every oil field in the world. Rest assured that oil is studied, measured, and projected ad nauseam. But, as I said before, somehow what makes the news is the story about a boy supposedly carried off in a balloon. When that happened in 2009, America stood still! That news headline—and every other triviality that comes along—routinely bumps any story about whether or not we have enough oil to fuel our lifestyles for the next ten years right off the airwaves.

What doesn't make the news is simply this. Every oil-producing country keeps track of its monthly and annual production. Production charts are available by well, field, country, the world, and for the U.S., by state from the EIA (Energy Information Association: www.eia.doe.gov), the statistical and analytical arm within the U.S. Department of Energy. Their job is to collect, analyze, and disseminate independent and impartial energy information in an effort to promote sound policymaking.

In graph after graph after graph prepared by the EIA, it is clear that oil production for any country, for any *field* in that country, resembles a bell-shaped curve. Production starts out low, then steadily increases, and then rapidly increases, until it plateaus or crests. Then it begins a steady and often rapid decline in production. This decline isn't because there is no oil left in the ground; rather, it is because what is left costs too much to extract. In other words, the cost of drilling and production exceeds the barrel price of the oil extracted. When that happens, the field and the wells are closed.

Oil companies, governments, consultants, and a variety of other technical experts spend a great deal of time and money trying to predict the peak of each well, field, country, and the world. In fact, long before the drill ever touches the ground, a proposed well has been analyzed up and down in an attempt to predict its production and profitability over the long term.

The hard part about all this is that, despite the testing and analyzing, it's next to impossible to know if any given well or field or country has attained its peak until it has started to decline. And that's bad news. What's worse is that our government is still acting like oil production is on the rise and not in decline. We are not preparing for a "what if" scenario. What if we have already hit the peak? By the time we know for sure, and if we haven't done anything in the meantime, it will be too late. This is not a wait-and-see, I'll-worry-about-that-tomorrow kind of issue. But our leaders are treating it like one.

People we call leaders are grappling with the minutia of this issue, instead of hedging all bets and saying, "We likely won't have oil as an energy source forever. Let's start weaning ourselves off it now. There may not be any rush, but there might be. And we don't want to risk the latter being true. Let's prepare instead of panic." Rather, we are graced with arguments surrounding issues like the following:

1) We can put new wells in existing fields; why worry? If production of one well drops, we drill another one. That boosts production. But for how long? And does it really boost production, or keep it the same?

2) New drilling technology will save us. It's hard to predict Peak Oil, because new technologies are coming along all the time that make once difficult-to-access oil now easy to extract. That boosts production, right? But can we keep outrunning the train?

3) Over- or under-stated production results. Oil drilling and production are in the hands of many people. There's no telling if production numbers are inflated or deflated, either by error or by design, to prove one point or another. I'd prefer to assume the worst on this one.

4) Depletion estimates are over- or under-stated. The formula for predicting the time of a future peak is inexact. The arguments, both technical and of the cocktail-party variety, are "lively" on both sides. Let's not focus on the speck of dust in the dust storm, okay?

Peak Oil for Individual Nations

In 2009, Wikipedia published statistics that show when various nations reached (or were projected to reach) Peak Oil. The data is easily supported by EIA data. The list is as follows:

Date	Country
1932	Japan
1966	Germany
1970	Libya, Venezuela, USA
1974	Iran
1979	Nigeria
1981	Trinidad, Tobago
1987	Egypt
1988	France
1991	Indonesia
1996	Syria
1997	India, New Zealand
1999	UK, Argentina, Columbia
2000	Australia (Production may rise for a peak in 2009), Norway, Oman
2004	Mexico
2006–07	Russia (May have peaked during this time period)

Estimated Peak

Date	Country
1973	Canada (Conventional)
2013	Kuwait
2014	Saudi Arabia
2018	Iraq
2020	Canada (Sands production)

Understandably, most companies and countries would prefer to have their peak as far in the future as possible. The perception of energy self-sufficiency is paramount to building a country's image of strength and stability. But in the U.S. there's no hiding the fact that our Peak Oil happened in 1970. Since then, our oil production has been in steady decline and our consumption has exponentially increased. As a result, we have had to import significant amounts of oil from virtually anyone who would sell it to us. Today, we import approximately 70 percent of our oil from foreign countries, many of which don't like us very much. We are at their mercy. Don't feel bad, though. We're in very good company.

Check out the country listed second from the bottom in the chart on the previous page. Any questions as to why we entered Iraq? The peaceful calm our nation experienced in terms of energy after World War II until the early 1970s is long gone. Low energy costs and a steady, uninterrupted supply of oil are luxuries of a bygone era. Today it's a different story. The 1980s, 1990s, and the 2000s have been rife with numerous upheavals, constant price increases, and many foreign-policy issues related to oil that have not been good for our world. With each decline in production—either real or fabricated for political motive—our economy and our wallets felt the pain.

But the pain we felt in the last few decades is nothing compared to the pain our world could feel if we experience even greater production declines. How quickly we forget the 1970s, when a modest 5-percent drop in production caused the price of oil to almost quadruple. Industry experts today predict that global production will continue to decrease from 3 to 10 percent each year due to reserve depletion, natural forces such as weather, and unnatural forces such as geo-political unrest. Add up those percentages and our global oil supply could be cut by as much as 50 percent in seven years. But don't take my word for it. Here's what Dick Cheney had to say about oil production in 1999 while he was the CEO of Halliburton:

"By some estimates, there will be an average of 2-percent annual growth in global oil demand over the years ahead, along with, conservatively, a 3-percent natural decline in production from existing reserves. That means by 2010 we'll need an additional 50 million barrels per day."

Andrew Gould, CEO of the giant oil services firm Schlumberger, concurs. He stated:

"An accurate average decline rate of 8 percent is not an unreasonable assumption."

Whether it is 3 or 5 or 8 or 10 percent, the reality is this: A drop in production will dramatically increase oil prices, which will have devastating effects on our world economy and our way of life. We know what happened in 1979, when the problem was temporary. Do we need to play it out again—fully unprepared—when our world and industry leaders saw the problem coming? Do we realize that, this time, the problem is permanent? If a production decline of 5 percent in the 1970s caused oil prices to almost *quadruple*, what will a production decline of 50 percent do to oil prices today or tomorrow? What will it do to our way of life? We should all shudder at the thought, and then pull ourselves together do something about it.

The Peak Oil argument is not one of "running out" of oil so much as it is not having enough to meet demand and keep our world economy going. The scariest part is that we won't need to hit bottom before we feel the pain of production decline. We'll feel it long before all the oil is used up. Some experts estimate that even a 10 to 15 percent drop in production could destroy our economy and launch us all into poverty.

Although experts have differing views about when Peak Oil will occur, it doesn't really matter. What matters is the steady decline, which is already underway. Some people who don't believe the peak is past us feel we'll reach the peak sometime between now and 2012.

After 2012, we could have production very similar to whatever we had at the peak, for several years. If you are breathing a sigh of relief, don't get too comfortable—because if you think those projections give us time to find alternatives, they don't. Here's why.

World Oil Consumption Levels

We are oil junkies. The world consumes approximately eighty million barrels of the stuff every day. The United States uses 25 percent of that (or twenty million barrels per day), and we import approximately 67 percent from other countries. In recent years, world oil production slightly exceeded the actual world consumption. The trouble is, consumption keeps increasing.

Right before our eyes, two countries—China and India—are growing up and earning their place in the modernized world. China's gross national product is rising 6 to 9 percent per year, and India's is not far behind. China is bringing several new coal-fired power plants online each month and buying gas-powered cars like there is no tomorrow. In fact, China is the biggest auto market in the world, and it is projected to grow its consumption of oil by 7 percent annually. India is right in there and also will have a significantly increasing need for oil. Is it possible, when the world returns to a positive economy, that we will outrun our oil supply? Will it take three years? Six? Ten? Maybe fewer? I think so—particularly when industry experts project production to decline year after year.

I believe our dependence on fossil fuel is the biggest problem we face as a nation and as a world economy. That's why I am addressing it first in this book. I wish the members of Congress and the White House were as concerned about our energy prognosis as I am. If they were, I am sure they would have a comprehensive energy policy already in place and passed.

The response of many congressional and White House people is that they have an energy policy; it's called Cap and Trade. They feel our energy problem will be handled by limiting carbon emissions. Here's the problem: It's not going to work. Cap and Trade is a *tax* bill, not an *energy* bill. It addresses the *symptoms* of the problem, not the source of the problem. The source of the problem is our reliance on fossil fuel for most of our energy. Why can't they see we need to save our energy supply by moving away from fossil fuels? Is our Democratic Congress so in bed with Big Oil that they, too, are playing into their hand? There's going to come a day when even Big Oil will realize they need a new game. But by that time it may be far too late for us to have any game at all.

If you are not concerned by all this, you are either really tough or brain dead (no offense). However, never fear. In the following sections we will review where our oil is used, and reveal a simple entrepreneurial plan to survive a transition to other energy sources.

Everything Requires Oil

According to AlternativeEnergyProcon.org, the four sectors of our economy use oil in the following percentages:

- Commercial (which includes retail, office, and warehouse buildings)—2 percent
- Residential (which includes homes and apartments)—3 percent
- Industrial (which includes agriculture, manufacturing, mining, and construction)—25 percent
- Transportation (which includes the cars we drive, shipping, freight, and air travel)—70 percent

When we think of oil consumption, it is easy to think only about the fuel that powers our cars. But the fact is that it takes oil to manufacture everything we see, touch, and consume. In many cases, it is a part of the products themselves. In a recent article written by Rachel Oliver and published by CNN, she shows just how much oil it takes to power our lives:

"In the U.S., up to 20 percent of the country's fossil fuel consumption goes into the food chain, which points out that fossil fuel use by the food system 'often rivals that of automobiles.' To feed an average family of four in the developed world uses up the equivalent of 930 gallons of gasoline a year—just shy of the 1,070 gallons that family would use up each year to power their cars."

These figures are not surprising when you realize that same article revealed that the average piece of food in the U.S. travels 1,500 miles before it makes it to your plate. So a reduction in oil production (even ever so slight) while consumption increases will not only affect our ability to get from home to the grocery store. It will affect the goods that are available at the store itself—in a big way. Has our government considered this fact? If they haven't, they need to start—and quick. But hedging that bet, I call the entrepreneurs of America to the front lines of what we'll call Operation: Fossil Fuel Freedom. We can't wait for the government. The future is in our hands. Here's one plan.

Create a Strong Future in Electrical and Biofuel Energy

Our country's future, (and nobody can tell me we do not have one), is dependent on our ability to shift to electrical and biofuel energy. Biofuels come from living organisms or from metabolic by-products like food waste. A fuel is a biofuel if it contains more than 80 percent renewable materials. I advocate biofuel for a few very obvious reasons:

- Using biofuel does not require any radical infrastructure changes, so it can be implemented easily.
- Biofuel is cheaper than fossil fuels.
- Biofuel is renewable and can be produced anywhere, so it reduces our dependence on fossil fuels.
- Of course, biofuel is better for the environment, even though it does take energy to produce it.

The good news is that biofuel is not new technology. We have a good start on this. Many of the solutions have been in the works for several years. We just need to pick up the pace and make sure we focus on projects that bring biofuel to the people in next three to seven years.

Drill, Baby, Drill

Yes, I did indicate in the beginning of this chapter that this cannot be our only solution, and I still hold my ground on that. But we need to make this energy transition as smooth as possible. The "drug" of oil will be one that will have plenty of withdraw symptoms if we are not careful. If "drill, baby, drill" can extend our production capacity by a few months or a few years, it will definitely help the transition. But we can't wait three or four years to do it; we must start now.

Transform Transportation

Since 70 percent of our fossil-fuel consumption goes to transportation, this must be a big area of focus, and soon. This includes cars, small trucks, sixteen-wheel semis, motorcycles, boats, and other recreational vehicles. Here's the plan:

- **Cars**—There are some hybrid models now. We must transition nearly all cars to hybrid within the next three to four years. From there, the transition to full electric vehicles must take place within five years. In other words, gas-powered cars will no longer be for sale by 2016.
- **Trucks**—Same thing as cars. For small trucks, we need to make the transition to hybrid on the same timetable as cars. Then transition them to all electric or, for heavy-duty trucks, biofuel.
- **16-wheel Semis**—There are already hybrid vehicles available. Transition to biofuel within five years, sooner if supply is available.
- **Motorcycles, Boats, and other Recreational Vehicles**— Transition all to electric. No exceptions.

Power Up Our World

No longer can we depend on fossil fuels alone to power our homes, businesses, and factories. It's going to take a combination of energy sources to power our world. Here's how I see it:

- Use electrical power for commercial, residential, and industrial
  - Generate electrical power using solar, wind, geothermal sources
  - Allow existing nuclear plants to remain operational
  - Convert all coal plants to biofuel
  - Operate all of these concurrently

- What about aviation? We are a mobile society, and air travel is a way of life. We can continue to enjoy traveling, but not if we're dependent on fossil fuels. Here's the alternative: biofuel. Yes, that's the answer. What you may not know is that several airlines have performed successful test flights using biofuel. It works! The key to full implementation is fuel production. Once again, entrepreneurs, it's time to rise to the occasion. Corporations, you're not off the hook. It's time to build our future.

- Another important area is our military. When I was in the army, a major military axiom was "Do not run out of fuel." Trust me, the military will not run out of fuel. There are too many smart people working on this project, and they are already testing significant amounts of biofuel. They are on it!

We'll Have to Give a Little

I saved this section for last, mainly because it is the most controversial. Of course, that statement assumes you agree with everything I've posed so far. Change is never easy, and weaning ourselves off of fossil fuels will be a very big change. It will not be without some pain for us all. But reality is reality, and if we go into this thing with our eyes open, the pain can be minimized. On the plus side, the result can be awesome! Think burgeoning new industries that catapult our economy forward in a very big way. That can happen, but first, here are the brutal facts:

- **Clean Coal**—I have tremendous respect for the miners of America. They are hard-working, brave men and women. But they have to get their management teams off the dime. If clean coal or coal-to-liquids is a viable energy source, then they have to do more than just pay it lip service. They need to start producing it and get it out there. Not sooner, not later, but *now!* Otherwise coal will have a difficult future. With as much supply as we have in the ground, it would be best to use it. And the "clean" part? It truly has to be clean.

- **Cap and Trade**—Congress could surely come up with a better plan than this. They are trying to tax everyone who uses an energy source that is unfavorable. Wouldn't it be much simpler to tax the manufacturer of the unfavorable energy source? Of course that probably would not work; it is too simple. The bill would only be about twenty pages long, and Congress is accustomed to 1,000- to 1,400-page behemoths.

- **Hydrogen Fuel Cell Technology**—This energy source has great potential, but it is slow to market. Not because there aren't products developed, but because the technology might not be cost-effective for five to ten years.

- **New Nuclear Plants**—It takes about four to eight years (or longer) to get the necessary permits to build a new plant. Then it takes another four to six years to build. Is that a timetable we can afford? I don't think so. And no one wants a cooling tower in his or her backyard. In addition, the cost of a nuclear plant is out of sight—around $10 billion or more! Before you see nuclear energy as a solution and consider building a new plant, do two quick studies. Find out if the plant will be able to get all the uranium it will need. The likelihood is that it will find its uranium fuel source becoming rapidly depleted. Nuclear energy may land us in the same predicament we have with oil. Then do a cost comparison. Really, it costs $10 billion? That will buy you a pretty big biomass fuel farm.

- **Finally, a Hot Business Tip**—Get in on the front end of a high-growth business opportunity! Think about this. With approximately 200 million or more cars in the U.S., and electricity or biofuel being the apparent winners in the alternative fuel race, there will be a market—a big market—for conversions. You could be the next Bill Gates. A computer on every desk? No, a conversion kit for every car! That's big bucks. With change comes massive opportunity for those who are willing to embrace it!

Summary

You may disagree with the Peak Oil concept, and I understand. But it's here, and unless we act, our country and perhaps the world will be hurting. The prognosis of what happens if we run out of oil without an alternative source is not pretty; in fact, it is awful. I have confidence we will not let that happen. I am counting on the American spirit to lead us through this crisis. We cannot count on the White House or Congress to do this for us. This is too important to turn over to people who have proven they do not listen to us, or care what we think about the issues of the day. This is up to *us*.

If you are a business person, an entrepreneur, a stockholder, a concerned American citizen, or someone ticked off because you have had no input in the future of our nation and our world, then the time to act is now. You can get involved by asking everyone with whom you come in contact what their short-term (three-year) and long-term (five-year) energy strategy is, and whether or not they are hitting their targets. The first few people you ask will probably look at you like you either just flew in from Mars or dropped off the turnip truck. Do not give up; keep asking them. Then delve a little further, and ask them what they would do if America ran out of oil, or if gas climbed to $8.99 a gallon. I think then they will listen, at least for a while. Maybe even think. And they'll ask someone else. The dialog and the demand for solutions will begin. In the meantime, don't fight change. Encourage it and own it. Invest in it. Talk about it. Write about it. And conserve.

Don't forget to enjoy yourself, though, and get a few laughs now. Because if we do not get this energy issue addressed, things will get very serious, very soon.

★★★★★★★★★★★★★★★★★★★★★★★★★

CHAPTER 3

SAVING HEALTH CARE

The Hippocratic Oath
Says "Do No Harm."
Treat our country
with identical respect.

The World Health Organization may not rank the American health care system as number one (in fact, it ranks us at number 37), but ask the person who has traveled from Canada, England, Italy, or a host of other countries for care in the United States and you'll come to learn that, despite the numbers, America is recognized as having the best health care in the world. And why wouldn't we? We have the most highly regarded medical schools, the best-trained physicians, the most technologically advanced hospitals, and the most sophisticated payer alternatives.

As patients, we have the freedom of choice. Yes, we can choose our physician and, if we are not happy, we can choose another. Our system offers advanced centers for specific diseases that are world-renowned. The Mayo Clinic and The University of Texas M.D. Anderson Cancer Center come to mind, and so does St. Jude Children's Research Hospital in Memphis, Tennessee. American health care even provides outstanding treatment for chronic diseases. Know anyone with kidney disease or who is coping with chronic pain? In America there is no waiting list for dialysis treatment, and there are a variety of pain treatment centers all ready and waiting to care for people in need. We also have emergency rooms, ambulance services, the 911 emergency system, and even urgent care walk-in clinics popping up on street corners and in drug stores all over the country.

Yes, for all the talk about American health care not measuring up, I just don't see it. And I *really* don't see it when I consider the outstanding support that our nurses, physical therapists, respiratory technicians, radiology technicians, and other practitioners who make up our health care system provide. There is no doubt in my mind that the American system, when compared with the systems of other countries, is far superior and would win any ranking system that truly measured care. The trouble is, the World Health Organization doesn't measure care. It measures five other factors and weighs them accordingly:

1. Health Level: 25 percent

2. Health Distribution: 25 percent

3. Responsiveness: 12.5 percent

4. Responsiveness Distribution: 12.5 percent

5. Financial Fairness: 25 percent

There's a fantastic article on the subject called *Popular Ranking Unfairly Misrepresents the U.S. Health Care System.* It covers in great detail this well-known and much-publicized ranking system biased toward socialized medicine. You can find it online, and it supports exactly what I am saying here. The article even cites a news story about Belinda Stronach, former liberal member of the Canadian Parliament and Cabinet member, who opted out of Canada's health care system— one deemed far better than ours in America by the World Health Organization—to undergo her cancer treatment in California. And if you dig a little deeper, you find out that when Italian Prime Minister Silvio Berlusconi needed *his* cancer treatment, he didn't head to a hospital in number-2 ranked Italy, he came to a Cleveland clinic. Have you ever seen a pro athlete needing a career-saving operation fly to (number 5) Malta or (number 4) Andorra to have it done? Of course not! That pro will have it done in America. Gee, World Health Organization, I guess old number 37 must be doing *something* right. Let's accept the fact that America has the best health care in the world.

So just what makes up that health care system? In its most basic form, the industry comprises providers, payers, patients, and suppliers. Within the industry we have more intellectual capability, meaning pure brainpower, than any other industry. Of course, all physicians have advanced degrees, and so do all other providers, many with PhDs. The industry represents several million people who are the country's best-educated and trained cadre of personnel. As a group, they also are one of the most dedicated to their profession.

There is also no shortage of well-educated and intellectual people who run hospitals and insurance companies. The same government agencies that contract the services of entrepreneurial firms such as EDS, Perot Systems, GTE, or IBM are even staffed by very intelligent and creative people. They *have* to be, in order to survive in an extremely competitive market. The question is: Are all these leaders putting their intellect to the best use?

The way I see it—having been a part of the health care industry for many years as the founder and CEO of a company called CyCare—the health care system, because of its size, has several major problems. Problems that have been with us for quite some time. The debate continues in the public and in the media about exactly how we should go about fixing those problems. Everyone has an opinion and, as you may have guessed, I have one, too. So does the U.S. Congress. They would like to completely overhaul health care in this country and, at this writing, are considering doing just that, in spite of fact that in an NBC/*Wall Street Journal* poll, 47 percent of people surveyed thought it was a bad idea, and only 32 percent said it was a good idea. Even without the majority of Americans feeling an overhaul is a good idea, our representatives in Congress just may pass a sweeping health care reform bill anyway.

Now I'm not saying we're perfect; health care in America certainly has plenty of room for improvement. But why not view health care as something that *almost* works and focus on the problem areas? Why overhaul the system *completely*? I'm at a loss here, particularly when the proposed system will *not* reduce overall health care costs. Here's what Robert A. Book, Senior Research Fellow in Health Economics at The Heritage Foundation, had to say during a recent PBS interview:

> *"The reforms currently in Congress will increase health insurance premiums and health care spending, not decrease them. The Lewin Group estimates that annual premiums will increase by an average of $460 per person—that's before taking into account coverage 'mandates' that the new Health Choices Commissioner would impose. Each of these mandates would increase premiums even more by forcing everyone to have 'Cadillac' plans or nothing.*

> *"In addition to this spending increase in the private sector, the Congressional Budget Office estimates that federal spending would increase by $1.3 trillion over 10 years. States would spend more because of additional Medicaid expansion.*

> *"Despite the rhetoric, the health care bills being debated contain nothing that 'incentivizes' the best treatments over the most expensive, or encourages healthier lifestyles. In fact, the Senate bill prohibits discounts for non-smokers. The focus on preventive care is welcome because it may improve health and save lives. But with few exceptions, it doesn't save money."*

According to some, the health care plan will not improve quality, either. Jim Martin, president of the 60 Plus Association, commented on National Public Radio (NPR) about this issue and how it relates to seniors. This is what he sees in the future if the health care bill passes:

> *"...the reform currently being proposed is devastating to the health care of most seniors in our country, and is about as helpful as placing the steps to the Philadelphia Art Museum in front of their doctors' offices. President Obama has proposed adding tens of millions of new people to a government health care plan, while cutting*

Medicare by over $500 billion. Meanwhile no new doctors will be added. It is clear that as government obligations grow and resources shrink, seniors will be most harmed."

Of course quality will suffer, and not just for seniors, but for everyone. The simple laws of supply and demand tell us so. What Congress is doing is ludicrous. This kind of activity makes clear why Congress has such a sterling favorable rating. What is it now? About 18 percent? Congress obviously feels they know what is best for America. It just makes you feel warm and fuzzy all over knowing we have leadership in Washington who, without any input from the citizens, knows what is best for us. When we talk about representative government, that's not really what we had in mind.

Regardless of which way the pending decision goes, whether they pass the bill or don't pass it, this chapter identifies seven problems plaguing health care which, when solved, would make most of the other problems we face with health care disappear.

Use this chapter to evaluate the congressional health care bill (if it passes), or use it to help write a new bill if the one in question does *not* pass. I believe implementing the following solutions to the seven problems plaguing health care will reduce costs and improve quality.

Seven Problems Plaguing Health Care

1. Antiquated Medical Records Systems
2. Excessive Cost of Malpractice
3. Health Insurance Doesn't Work for Everyone
4. The Wrong People Control Your Health Care
5. Cost Control Incentives Don't Exist
6. Insurance Premiums Are Too High for Many People
7. Health Care is Not Accessible to Everyone

Problem: Antiquated Medical Records Systems
Solution: The Electronic Medical Chart

The current status of the patient medical chart in a majority of medical practices is one of utter chaos and inefficiency. The paper medical chart has reached the end-point of its usefulness and effectiveness. Approximately half of all larger group practices have already implemented electronic medial charts, but only about 25 percent of the smaller groups have upgraded their systems. They are still using manual paper-based documents. You've seen them. They're the ones enclosed in a manila folder with a colorful label on the outside. There's one for each patient and they're stored in a file room. In some offices, I've seen piles of charts sitting here or there waiting to be updated or filed—and, frankly, it's not very comforting. This system, given the current workload and the complexity of most practices today, is an accident waiting to happen. The room for error is enormous.

What we have is a medical records system designed for practices caring for a population one-fourth the size of the one we have today. It's a paper records system that was designed to manage care with technology and treatment protocols that seem downright primitive by today's standards. It's inefficient, costly, and is one of the big reasons why health care costs so much. Medicine is one of the most technologically advanced industries in almost every way, except when it comes to patient medical records management. There is something drastically wrong with that picture, and we patients are being short-changed. I don't know about you, but I'd rather have the money I pay for care going to actual *care*, not reams of paper and boxes of folders. Get rid of the files and you lower costs. Ask any group practice that has implemented electronic medical records. I don't know of a single one that has reverted to paper because the electronic system was costing them more.

In fact, a physician group practice can save an estimated 15 to 25 percent of operational costs annually by converting from paper charts to electronic medical records. That's a big number. Practices find those savings from improved personnel performance. Not only does it take fewer people to run the practice, but the people who *are* there can streamline their work and actually get more done. Electronic medical records also reduce transportation costs. We don't think about it, but every time X-ray films or entire charts must be transported to another physician or a hospital, it costs money, whether it is sent by courier or by an administrative person assembling the documents and feeding them through a fax machine.

In addition, what patient in need of care wouldn't want their records to be available in an instant to his primary care provider, his cardiologist, his urologist, and so forth? Don't you want the right hand knowing what the left hand is doing and prescribing? Have you heard of that scary little problem called drug interactions? Electronic medical records provide instant accessibility and have the power to prevent a lot of mistakes that could result in injury, death, and, of course, lawsuits.

As it stands now, your life is sitting in a folder with pages and pages of handwritten notes. When you are referred to another physician, a specialist, perhaps, your chart, if it is paper, needs to be hauled to several different staging areas within the practice and then sent to the new practice. This is slow by design, and even *slower* when you consider that only one person at a time can review or update the records. With an electronic chart and the appropriate security clearance, professionals caring for you can update or review the chart instantly, and several qualified people can do this simultaneously. Whether you know it or not, your chart is routinely viewed by dozens of people related to your care—including physicians, consulting physicians, nurses, schedulers, insurance processors, pharmacists, and prescription refill physicians. If you get referred to another physician, go to an emergency room, or get checked into a hospital, this list grows exponentially. Let's be blunt. Architects, contractors, and builders wouldn't *dream* of designing and building a structure with a single set of blueprints and no version control today. Why on earth do we stand for this kind of inept and accident-prone system for our health?

The efficiencies even go beyond the charting. With electronic medical records, physician practices and hospitals can electronically schedule patients, check them into facilities, record their medical visits into the chart, prescribe prescriptions, automatically generate the appropriate charges, and schedule any follow-up appointments. They can even print a follow-up schedule and protocol for the patient—all without generating any paper documents and in a fraction of the time it would take to do all that with paper and pen. In addition, the documents are legible (we are talking about physicians here, who are notorious for their poor penmanship) and available on a 24/7 basis.

Fortunately, during the last decade, several entrepreneurial companies have built and are installing electronic medical record systems. I'm glad to hear this is part of the health care reform bill and that President Obama has allocated funding for this. (I assume he will follow up on this campaign promise.) The problem is the naysayers out there, who are afraid that electronic medical records can reduce our privacy and be used against us. I have to actually laugh at that concern, because if you haven't realized by now, your medical records are already in the hands of hundreds of people, in black and white, and with no security codes, no encryption, no legitimate security whatsoever. If you think paper is secure, you are sadly mistaken. An electronic medical records system is inevitable, and the sooner every practice in this country is fully integrated into the system, the faster we will all see the benefits in terms of convenience, cost savings, and, most importantly, care. Let's move on this!

Problem: Excessive Cost of Malpractice
Solution: Health Care Tort Reform

How perfect that our next discussion is about malpractice, because I often wonder exactly how many errors that lead to malpractice suits are caused by antiquated medical record keeping. While we all talk about how the cost of health care has increased during the last few years (we all feel that directly), few of us fully know how the cost of malpractice insurance has skyrocketed. Unless we are physicians, we don't experience that pain—and painful it is. Most of us know of at least one physician who has decided to either close a practice or limit it because the cost of insurance is just too high. Obstetricians have been in the news over the years as those among the hardest hit. Not only is it a shame that a physician can't do his or her work and make a reasonable living, but this whole situation is, once again, reducing the quality of our care.

Tort reform advocates like me believe that putting into effect a federal law limiting such things as legal fees, punitive damages, and non-economic (pain and suffering) damages in malpractice cases is the right thing to do. According to the National Conference of State Legislatures, many states have laws of some sort governing medical liability lawsuits. For example, typically there is a two-year statute of limitations for standard medical malpractice claims, and more than half the states already have limits on damage awards. But what about states that don't? And what about states with laws on their books that don't go far enough to really deter frivolous lawsuits that can reap big financial rewards for undeserving patients and overly ambitious attorneys?

In Texas, where they have initiated more aggressive health care tort reform, the governor's office reported a 27-percent drop in the cost of malpractice insurance. According to the *Wall Street Journal*, "In the last three years, 7,000 doctors have moved to Texas. So many doctors want to practice there that the state has had trouble keeping up with the volume of requests for licenses." Hmm—sounds to me like they have some smart people in Texas. I wonder if they could get a few more of them to run for the U.S. Congress.

Don't get me wrong. If a physician does something wrong and the result of that error is illness, injury, or death, the patient (or the family of that patient) should have the right to seek legal action if they so desire. The purpose of health care tort reform is to bring some reasonability back into the system. We are not trying to eliminate malpractice claims, but rather put a reasonable lid on the non-economic punitive damage awards of those claims.

Problem: Health Insurance Doesn't Work for Everyone
Solution: Reform the Insurance System

Please don't count me among those people who think that private insurers should be completely eliminated, because I don't believe they should. But I *do* believe they could be doing a lot of things better than they are, and serving all the people who need to be served in the process. There is a lot of room for improvement, but there are three areas in particular that, if solved, would take care of many of the others.

The first issue is how to insure people with preexisting conditions. In our current health insurance environment, a person who has a preexisting condition will either not qualify for insurance, be classified as a risk and be forced to pay ridiculously high premiums, or be insured at slightly lower rate but with an exclusionary rider for the exact condition for which they may need the insurance. It's no win, no win, and no win.

There are people today with preexisting conditions who are trapped in jobs they hate because those jobs provide insurance coverage—or, worse yet, they no longer have jobs that provided insurance and are now not only facing loss of their income, but also the loss of their health coverage. When these people, employed or unemployed, try to get new coverage, either the premiums will drive them to bankruptcy, or the uncovered medical expenses will. This is not right in our country. The insurance companies need to find a feasible method for underwriting people with preexisting conditions. If you don't agree with me on this point, then this sad situation either hasn't happened to you or it hasn't happened to anyone you care about, at least as far as you know. But wait. Unless this is fixed, it's just a matter of time.

The second problem area is making health insurance coverage offerings more affordable to small businesses. Despite what many people think about business—that it is cold, heartless, and greedy—step back for a minute and realize that businesses are run by your neighbor, your sister, your brother, your cousin, your friends … maybe by you! Nasty, terrible ogres don't run these businesses. Many are operated by people just like you and me, who care very much about the lives of their employees. Many small businesses would gladly offer health insurance if they could do so at a reasonable cost.

Now, before you jump to the conclusion that all small businesses are putting profits over the health and well-being of their employees, allow me to clear up that notion right away with a story that is true, but not by any means unique. In fact it is the norm. A company I work with decided to offer health insurance to its six employees and began sourcing providers. It got bids and estimates from at least five different carriers. After a great deal of work and time, they decided on one insurer, Blue Cross Blue Shield. It cost the company more than $15,000 in premiums for the first year, because the company offered to pay 50 percent of each employee's monthly premium. But here's the startling part. That fee was only for the two employees who took the insurance. The other four found the monthly premiums—even with the company's 50 percent contribution—much higher than the premiums they were paying for private individual and family coverage.

Here's a company, like most, that wanted to do the right thing, but the insurance companies made it impossible. To add insult to injury, in the second year the insurer raised the premiums by 30 percent. In the third year the company terminated formal health insurance benefits and instead now helps their employees find personal coverage and then subsidizes it. Here again, we have a problem. But the solution is simple: Establish co-ops for small business groups. Why isn't this in place? Through a co-op, small businesses could join together and create a large enough employee base to receive the same premiums that larger companies with bigger employee bases enjoy. Not only does this make financial sense, but it makes business sense, too. In any insurance product, whether it is life insurance or property/casualty, it is always better to spread risk. Hey, if you're an insurance company that insures homes only in Key West, Florida, and a hurricane hits, it doesn't matter how high your premiums were. You're out of business. Co-ops spread risk, and when you spread risk, you can reduce premiums.

The third big problem is that insurance companies operate state by state and can't sell insurance across state lines unless they comply with the unique insurance laws in that state. Why is that a problem? Because it limits competition and makes it harder to spread risk, which, as I stated earlier, can reduce premium costs. If Americans could shop for insurance from a host of providers beyond the ones in their own backyard, natural market pressures would bring the costs down, and insurers would have to become more price competitive.

If you don't believe the power of this market force, consider telephone service. In the old days, we were at the mercy of one provider: Bell Telephone. Then the government ordered the breakup of Bell into what they called "Baby Bells." While there was an appearance of competition among these regional offshoots, there really wasn't. If you lived in Houston, you had to use Southwest Bell for your phone service; you couldn't price shop, realize Pacific Bell was cheaper and use them. When cellular phone technology arrived, everything changed. With cellular phones, you could buy from service providers that were nationwide. Anyone anywhere could buy—and can buy—from Verizon, Sprint, AT&T, and so forth. What happened to phone service prices? They went down, and they *keep* going down. Consumers benefited, and companies had to get leaner and smarter.

The same can happen for health insurance if we allow the free market to do what it does best: let the consumers vote with their wallets, and may the best companies win. As long as we artificially limit choice and restrict competition, the insurance companies are winning. After all, what incentive do I have as an insurance company to lower my prices if I have a captive consumer base? None! Allowing people to *shop* for insurance across state lines means insurers must be allowed to *sell* across state lines. When this happens, the result will be lower premiums for all.

Problem: The Wrong People Control Your Health Care
Solution: Put the Right People in Charge

So just who *are* the right people? Is it the insurance companies? No. That's pretty much who is in charge of your care now. Is it the government? No, but it likely will be if the health care bill passes. So who *should* be in charge of your care? That answer's easy: You and your physician.

Before you cheer, "Right on!" or pound your fist on the table and say, "Darn right!" recognize that with this right comes responsibility. Let's start with what being in charge of your health means. Sure, it's easy to think that when you're in control of your health care, you'll see the specialists you want to see when you want to see them, you'll get the tests, no matter the costs, whenever you want them and get the pills you need to make you do everything from sleep better to have better sex.

Sorry. That's not what being in charge of your health means. It means taking responsibility for your diet and your lifestyle. And that is something Americans have not been very good at doing over the last few decades. As a population, we overeat, we are overweight, and our health care system is buckling under the ballooning illnesses our horrible habits have created as we age.

As much as many Americans would like to deny the facts, there is a very strong correlation between lifestyle habits—including diet, exercise and smoking—and overall health. Some experts tell us that 95 percent of diabetes, hypertension, heart disease, and strokes could be eliminated by eating right, exercising, and throwing away the cigarettes. Give me a break, that cannot *possibly* be true! I know, you're either one of those naysayers or you *know* a few of those naysayers who roll their eyes and say, "I'll believe it when I see it." Well, you're seeing it every day. America, a country that has the best health care system in the world, is unhealthy because we don't take responsibility for our own health. All the technology in the world won't save us from ourselves. To make sure you get the most out of any health care system, start with good health, which means eat right, exercise, and, if you haven't already, stop smoking.

Point made. You are responsible for your health. But it is your *physician* who should be in charge of your health care, and right now he or she is not. Some say the health maintenance organizations (HMOs), insurance companies, or employers are in charge. Others feel the men and women who lead hospitals are the ones calling the shots. It doesn't matter who is actually in charge (it might very well be *all* of them at one time or another), the reality is that it should be *none* of them.

It's the physicians who simply must direct the care of their patients. They are trained to do this, and, in essence, it is what they are supposed to be doing. Ultimately, it is *you* who must decide to act on the recommendations of your physician or not, but it is your *physician* who should decide which tests to order, which drugs to prescribe, which hospital to admit you into, and what the appropriate course of treatment is for you. Yes, it's the physicians who should be in charge of health care, but unfortunately, in many cases, they are not.

Given my experience in this industry, it is all too apparent that in small practices and physician-owned group practices it is the physicians who are in charge, for the most part. However, when hospitals or insurance companies purchase the practice, a subtle but meaning-ful change takes place. Suddenly the physicians lose their autonomy, patient care becomes secondary to profits, and everyone loses, even the company that now owns the practice (if not in the short term, in the long term). Excellent service matters in medicine today, and that means keeping the physicians in charge.

In physician-owned groups, it is commonplace to have an admin-istration led by a physicians board. In corporate-led practices, it's com-mon to see an administration led by a business-oriented board. What is the difference? A physicians board will understand the importance of a health care communication system that has immediate access to all patient medical information. A business board will also understand that need, but will have a tendency to assign a lower priority to the project. Another view would state that a physicians board is going to be more inclined to focus on what made them successful in the first place, which is patient care, not patient business. To save health care, the physicians in the large corporate-owned practices need to reclaim their voice and their control of health care.

Problem: Cost Control Incentives Don't Exist
Solutions: Payer Programs

I could have easily included this problem among the other problems with the health insurance system, but because it has the potential to so dramatically reduce health care costs, I felt it deserved its own section in this book. In fact, many insurance companies are already tackling the problem and finding solutions in the form of payer programs. Think of them as incentives given to the people they insure to use health care prudently and take responsibility for their own wellness.

By every estimation, the health care industry is very unique. Unlike most industries, which have buyers and sellers, health care has three entities in the mix: provider, payer, and patient. This current system has one major structural problem: the patient has little to no incentive to control the costs of care. Think about it: If you have coverage with a $1,000 deductible, you'll be careful to limit your health care costs up to the $1,000. But let's say you needed knee surgery in February and you easily met your $1,000 deductible. Do you really care how much your health care costs the system for the remainder of the year? Of course you don't. You met your deductible, paid your monthly premiums, and if you need an MRI, you'll get the MRI—and maybe an ultrasound along with it for good measure. Why should you try to cut costs when someone else is already paying for it? After all, it's *your* health and this is why you have insurance.

The problem with that thinking is that for us, as a country, to control health care without rationing, we need an innovative way to involve the patient in controlling costs. The good news is that this system currently exists and is very popular with business insurance plans. It has many different names, including health savings accounts, but basically the way it works is quite simple. The business owner sets aside a portion, say 20 to 40 percent, of an employee's annual health insurance premium in a fund. That money is in the employee's name. The employee uses that fund to pay for medical services and treatments up to the amount of the fund. The insurance company pays for any charges over the amount that was set aside.

Here's the incentive part. At the end of the year, any dollars *not used* by employees are theirs to keep. Now we have an insurance system where the patient is vitally interested in reducing the cost of care. For perhaps the first time in America, we would have a nation of cost-conscious "consumers" of medical services. That's a system for our times. Everyone wins.

This is a very innovative and entrepreneurial way to control health care costs and give employees who have taken responsibility for their own health a way to acquire some additional equity.

Problem: Insurance Premiums Are Too High for Many People
Solution: Employer Funding of Health Insurance

Most large companies voluntarily provide health insurance to their employees and, as I mentioned earlier, some contribute all or part of the monthly premium as a benefit of employment. Although health care costs are rising nationally, several companies, through some very entrepreneurial programs, have been able to control health insurance costs for themselves and for their employees. Safeway is one company that has been very creative with their health insurance program. Steven Burd, CEO of Safeway Inc., and the founder of the Coalition to Advance Healthcare Reform, stated in the *Wall Street Journal's* "Opinion Journal" that Safeway has kept its per capita health care costs (that includes both the employee and the employer portion) flat over the last four years, while most American companies' health insurance costs have increased by 38 percent during the same period.

Just how did Safeway do it? Here's Burd's summary:

> *"Safeway's plan capitalizes on two key insights gained in 2005. The first is that 70% of all health care costs are the direct result of behavior. The second insight, which is well understood by the providers of health care, is that 74% of all costs are confined to four chronic conditions (cardiovascular disease, cancer, diabetes and obesity). Furthermore, 80% of cardiovascular disease and diabetes is preventable, 60% of cancers are preventable, and more than 90% of obesity is preventable. Our plan utilizes a provision in the 1996 Health Insurance Portability and Accountability Act that permits employers to differentiate premiums based on behaviors. Currently we are focused on tobacco usage, healthy weight, blood pressure and cholesterol levels."*

Safeway calls this their Healthy Measures program, and participation is completely voluntary. But surprisingly, or maybe not surprisingly, more than 74 percent of the insured non-union workforce has signed up. And why wouldn't they? Employees who pass all four tests can see their annual premiums lowered off a base premium by $780 for individuals and $1,560 for families. It's all confidential; management does not ever see an employee's test results.

There's no doubt that health care costs go down when people start taking responsibility for their own health, and companies like Safeway give people that little extra push they need to wise up. You might ask yourself why an employer would want to bother with offering health insurance or going the extra mile with a program like Healthy Measures. After all, there is expense involved. One of the reasons is because it is in the employer's best interest to take care of his or her employees. Modern management techniques teach the importance of taking care of your team. The American Management Association agrees that it is the CEO's responsibility to ensure that the company attracts the best personnel, trains the employees, and retains them. That's how you build a successful company: attract, train, and retain. Offering the best health benefits you can is a big part of that formula.

I believe it should be mandatory for all companies with fifty or more employees to offer a minimum insurance plan paid by the employer. For employers with less than fifty employees, I believe it should be mandatory to have some type of group plan, but the employer should have the flexibility they do now to determine the percentage they pay.

My positions on mandatory insurance for large businesses (over fifty employees) and optional participation on premiums for small businesses will probably irritate both the far right *and* the far left. Good! I am not too happy with them, either. But we've got to get real in this country, don't you think? Idealism on either side makes for great talk radio and is making some talk show hosts a lot of money, but it's not progressing our country.

One provision in the proposed health care bill is extremely harmful to the country's leading companies, and the reason I care is because it is critical that American companies stay competitive in our global marketplace. Remember, it's those companies that provide jobs. The provision states that companies with high-value health care packages will pay a penalty on their plans. That means companies like IBM, John Deere, and Northwestern Mutual, who have taken care of their employees, will be penalized. The natural response to stay competitive will likely be to pare down the plans, which only hurts the employees who have made those companies and America great. Why would anyone want to tear down those great businesses that have acted in the best interests of their employees and the country? Congress is taking the very best of us, and lowering our competitive effectiveness throughout the world. I just don't get that thinking—unless, of course, our elected officials are intent on destroying America! Let's not. We have a great country, incredibly successful businesses, and I would like to keep things that way.

Problem: Health Care is Not Accessible to Everyone
Solution: Provide Health Care Access to Everyone

When I speak of access, I'm really referring to two things. The first is the ability of a person to pay, and the second is the availability of care if a person is sick. By law, if someone is sick, hospital emergency rooms cannot refuse care; so access to the system is always available. In other words, that care is there even for people who do not have the ability to pay for it. Every year, hundreds of thousands are cared for by this societal safety net.

While no one will debate the fact that there are people out there who are uninsured, there is a lot of debate on how *many* uninsured people there are. Some say the number is as high as forty million people. But let's take a look at this further in light of my recommendations for saving health care. In this chapter I mention that our system needs to cover people who have preexisting conditions. I've also recommended that large companies be required to provide and pay for insurance plans, and that small companies be required to have a standard plan, but they could decide the percent of the employer-paid potion of the premium. COBRA is in place as a means to continue company health care coverage in the event of a loss of employment, and Medicaid is available for individuals who are unemployed.

Now, with all these programs—existing and proposed—who would be left that is uninsured? The answer is primarily young people who do not want to buy insurance. If you follow the logic in this section, you have to ask what will happen to the forty million uninsured people the politicians like to talk about? Is it possible that the theoretical forty million uninsured people would shrink to less than *one* million uninsured people if we implemented the recommendations identified in this chapter? Hmm…

My math has been fairly good, although I do not have the exact numbers for my plan from the certified plan evaluator or the Congressional Budget Office (CBO), however, neither does Congress or the White House. We have seen health care reform plan estimates ranging from $900 billion to $2.5 trillion for ten years of the new plan. That's quite a spread. I really hope you feel more comfortable with these numbers than I do. In fact, if you agree with even these White House and congressional projections, as vague as they are, I have a bridge I would like to sell you. It's in Brooklyn, and its big—really, really big. Probably needs a little work.

Summary

Electronic medical records, tort reform, insurance company reform, patient control of health and physician control of care, payer programs, employer-funded health care, and access to all are the solutions we must implement. I doubt that putting these solutions in place would cost taxpayers more than one-tenth of the government's proposed plan. I know it would expand care and improve quality while it bends the cost curve. Now, I realize that doing something that would actually benefit the taxpayers would be a first for Congress of late, but there is no time like the present. And we all know at some point they are going to want to become involved with the citizens (commonly referred to as voters). If not now, when?

CHAPTER 4

SAVING ENTREPRENEURSHIP

Whatever we can imagine
Can be accomplished.
Turn the entrepreneur loose
And everyone will benefit.

Consider this chapter an appeal to save the entrepreneurs of America. Whether you consider yourself one or not, understand entrepreneurs are in jeopardy, and so are their businesses. That impacts us all because today, we need entrepreneurs more than ever. They are responsible for creating more jobs than any other group in our country, and it is they, the energized few, who see problems and go against the grain to fix them. I think you will all agree that we have more than a few problems to fix in our society and the world. Many of the most daunting ones are in this book. And the ones that aren't can probably be fixed by curing the ones discussed in these pages.

If you are not an entrepreneur, you might consider skipping this chapter. I hope you don't. You never know when you may find yourself embarking upon a home-based business or starting a company. The information and the recommendations in this chapter will help you. And besides, it's time for us all to wake up and get involved. We cannot afford to be quiet anymore. Perhaps you will appreciate this:

They came for my neighbor,
I did not protest.
They came for my banker,
I did not protest.

> *They came for me,*
> *I protested violently.*
> *But it was too late.*
> *My singular voice was not enough.*

Right now, it's not too late. But if we stay passive, it will be. I have spent my life as an entrepreneur, as well as a mentor to and investor with entrepreneurs. I have authored two books, *Seize the American Dream: 10 Entrepreneurial Success Strategies* and *Grow the Entrepreneurial Dream: How to Take Your Business From Start-Up to World-Class*, that teach people how to build and grow successful entrepreneurial companies. And I have spent my life practicing what I preach. I write this chapter not to share the secrets of business success, but to preserve innovation, capitalism, and the American way of life. Each of these is under attack right now, right under our noses. We have the White House, its staff of czars, and the United States Congress to thank for it. I equate our charge right now to a major battle and long war for our freedom as individuals and citizens.

Where do I get these notions? I read the news and listen to the rhetoric. I evaluate both sides of the arguments, but invariably, it appears to me President Obama is more interested in income redistribution and moving us to a Socialist society than he is in preserving our way of life. This chapter's purpose is to enlist as many citizens as possible in the quest for saving America, especially the entrepreneurs and small business owners of this country. It will take every one of us—business owners or not—to keep the backbone of America strong enough to support our future.

The American Way

Take a look at history. Whether it be the westward migration through railroads, the communications revolution with the birth of the telephone, or the dawn of information through the invention of the computer, the key to America's growth during the last 200 years can be directly attributed to the free enterprise system. We have experienced the origination of several million companies, significant gross domestic product (GDP) growth, product leadership in almost all market segments, tremendous marketing innovations, and millions of jobs in the American economy. Entrepreneurs have been responsible for putting food on every table in America in one way or another.

The vast majority of these companies were started and funded by people with a dream and a vision who possessed persistence in the face of many failures to bring an idea to life. They used their own money and bootstrapped their way to success. I believe that less than 10 percent of business successes began with funding by venture capitalists or angel investors. In the process, billions have been made and lost—that's part of the game.

It's true, many entrepreneurs fail, repeatedly, before they ever succeed. I've heard that as many as 85 percent of businesses fail within the first five years. But true entrepreneurs are a very resilient bunch, and a high percentage start over again and again if necessary until they win. Walt Disney is said to have gone through bankruptcy several times before becoming successful with Mickey Mouse, Donald Duck, and Goofy. Milton S. Hershey filed for bankruptcy after several failed ventures before starting the Hershey Chocolate Company. Even Abraham Lincoln filed for bankruptcy when his grocery business failed. He pressed on to become a lawyer and, of course, one of our most illustrious and admired presidents. Entrepreneurs persist.

The Two Who Understood

John F. Kennedy and Ronald Reagan—one a Democrat, the other a Republican—have been, in my estimation, the best of the thirteen presidents I've experienced in my lifetime. Interestingly enough, they both entered office in similar economic times. They each had to deal with an economy in a recession, high inflation, high interest rates, and the Cold War. Both men were pro-business. To solve these problems, Kennedy lowered taxes and initiated a 10-percent investment tax credit to stimulate the economy. He also handled a major showdown with Russia that involved Cuban missiles. Reagan also lowered taxes, and he built a strong military. He, too, handled a major crisis that involved the continual threat of nuclear war and won the Cold War through innovation without firing a shot. They understood the importance of entrepreneurs and were, in a way, entrepreneurial themselves.

When Kennedy was president, I was a sales representative for IBM, and the investment tax credit created a strong impetus for businesses to buy or lease new equipment. It was great! Business boomed and America took a huge step forward in technology leadership. When Reagan was president, I was CEO of CyCare Systems. I will never forget his comments about entrepreneurs: "This is the age of entrepreneurs; it's the entrepreneurs who create the new products, create the new jobs, and help America grow." Both men were extremely inspiring, both were on our side against the government, both made us feel great about being an American, and both leveled with or told the truth to the American people. Sounds almost like a fairy tale by recent standards, doesn't it? I was there, it's the truth.

I know, I know, having a politician who actually levels with us, tries to actually fulfill his campaign promises, is something different then what we are experiencing today. I'm not complaining, and I fully plan to work within the system to make the best of the situation we've got. Like many people have said, it's time to "buckle up your chin strap and tough it out!" Well, tough it out to me doesn't mean just standing by. Entrepreneurs aren't like that, nor are CEOs. I qualify as both.

Silence is Golden

Here's why it's so hard for me to sit back and do nothing. Consider the following track record, all of which affects you, me, business, and America:

Tarp (Troubled Asset Relief Program)

This was a $790-billion fund set up to help banks weather a recession and stave off a possible depression. All the money was supposed to be paid back to the government and reduce the deficit. Some banks have actually paid back the money, along with interest. Now President Obama has decided he wants to use the dollars for other purposes. In other words, set up a slush fund for the president and Treasury Secretary Tim Geithner. That wasn't part of the deal, and I have heard no real justification for this shift of strategy. Maybe they have a Vegas trip planned?

Stimulus Package

This $700-billion fund was put in place to stimulate the economy and keep unemployment from going above 8 percent. In December 2009, unemployment was above 10 percent and, rumor has it, a significant portion of the stimulus was used for partisan constituent payoffs. That is really nice. Where exactly did this money go? As a CEO, I'd like to see the expense report. I'm not so sure I would approve all of the expenditures.

Energy Cap and Trade

Does the U.S. have any energy policy? I don't think so, we should be attempting to produce as much oil as possible, but are we? No! Cap and Trade, a program in which the federal government sets a limit or "cap" on carbon emissions in a given area and then allows firms or individuals to trade carbon credits to meet the cap, is a joke. Actually it's a disgrace, because it is nothing more than a tax bill; a vehicle for the government to tax everyone for everything. My earlier chapter on energy covers the need to address the source of the problem and find solutions.

American Business Takeover

Beyond the questionable government programs, so many industries in America are being tampered with in Washington, it's hard to keep track of them all. Here are a few more visible ones that are on the government's hit list to either favor or fault:

Banking

Let's talk about banks. Did you know the government has the power to shut down just about any bank whenever it desires? It's the government that tells banks they must make sub-prime loans, or be restricted in their growth, or have their capital position re-evaluated. If they fail to comply with government mandates, they lose their charter. That's every bank except the ones deemed too big to fail. Yes, the Federal Reserve is protecting the fifteen to twenty largest banks in America.

Mortgage Loans

Thanks to the government's ownership of Fannie Mae and Freddie Mac, home loans under $600,000 are pretty much with and guaranteed by the federal government, or the taxpayers. The government owns the industry. There is and will be little room for other private-sector players.

Car Manufacturing

Do you want the government in the car business, or in business at all? Think back to the bailout transaction. General Motors was worth about $1 billion in the marketplace. The government paid $50 billion to keep GM in business. Then GM went into bankruptcy, the government ended up with 60 percent of the company's stock (which is now worth next to nothing), and stands no chance of ever being worth even close to what the government spent on the bailout. This is the epitome of a bad deal.

Radio Stations

At one point the federal government had a plan to establish a series of public radio stations. They planned on having existing private stations fund the public stations by simply paying a significant portion of revenues to the federal government. If any station chose not to participate, its license could be revoked. Doesn't sound like America to me. Makes you wonder what the White House will come up with next.

Aviation

If the White House had a plan to screw over aviation, they could not have done a better job of destroying the industry. I do not think they had a particular plan; they just made so many uninformed comments about business jet users that they created an incorrect and maligned perception of business aviation. You may be surprised to know companies that use business aviation have higher growth rates than those that do not. You may also be surprised to know that for public companies who use business aviation, their return on equity is approximately 45 percent higher than those public companies that are non-users. It's not just a bunch of bigwigs flying around the world on the company's dime, but that's the perception, thanks to our government and the media.

The Internet

Okay, this should scare the daylights out of you. Congress is attempting to pass legislation that will allow the federal government to take over the Internet in an emergency. That would give them control of almost every industry, every line of communication, every particle of information, and every bit of free speech. And who declares something an emergency? The same people who have the keys to the vault. Wow. This one will stop you in your tracks.

There are others. These are just a few examples.

Last But Not Least...

There are a few other factors that make if difficult for me to just sit this one out. The first is White House czars. Why do we need thirty-seven or more czars in the White House? Who approves their actions, and who approves their hiring? The next is the limited business experience that exists in the White House. Without a doubt, running a country is very much like running a big business—it takes experience. That's something this administration of Ivy-League grads is sorely lacking.

They have community organizing experience, but that's not enough.

Speaking of enough, have *you* had enough? What are you going to do to get things back in balance? How about we work my action plan to help empower American business and entrepreneurs?

Empowerment Plan for American Business and Entrepreneurs

Here's the Kennedy/Reagan/Houtz (if I could be so bold) recommendation to spur the American economy, create jobs, and keep the government from taking over our lives and our livelihoods:

1. Significantly lower taxes on the first $200,000 of annual income for small businesses with less than 500 employees.

2. Establish a 10-percent business investment tax credit on all leased or purchased equipment for all business entities.

3. Lower taxes on the first $1 million of annual income for all business entities that manufacture or assemble products in the United States.

4. Dramatically expand the SBA (Small Business Administration) loan availability.

5. Develop an employee-hiring bonus that gives the employer an amount equal to 20 percent of first-year compensation for each new employee the company hires.

Each and every one of these solutions would spur entrepreneurial investment and ignite growth. These solutions would be a real stimulus. I know, you are thinking, "This all seems too simple."

If our government would implement these suggestions, I am convinced they would turn the economy around. They are simple, on purpose, and are something Congress can understand. Heaven knows, their performance in the last decade demonstrates that we need to make things as easy for them to understand as possible. And now that we have a plan, what will it take to help them expedite it? It will take action from all of us. Here are your marching orders to save America:

- Stay or become involved in the Tea Parties.

- Participate in consumer or business groups (or both).

- Promote fiscal responsibility in our government by discussing our concern about current spending levels at the Tea Parties and with members of Congress and their staffs.

- Become involved in the 2010 elections and vote out the incumbents, particularly those who have shown no fiscal restraint and responsibility. Don't vote party lines—vote big spenders out!

American entrepreneurs are the least demanding of almost all special interest groups. We are not looking for a handout or a grant. We expect to earn whatever we get. We start or grow our business based on perceived opportunities. There are more than two million of us out here, looking for opportunities and searching for problems that need solving.

When we decide to start or grow our business we do not look at tax rates, various government grants, or capital gains rates. We are looking for a level and consistent playing field. It is particularly irksome when the government or, more specifically, the White House, anoints some product or industry group with grant dollars (our tax money, or Chinese loans), which in effect awards their selection as the winner instead of letting the marketplace make that determination.

Entrepreneurs want to see some stability in the current government regulations. Growing businesses like that, although instability will not stop entrepreneurs. Promoting health care or Cap and Trade while ignoring unemployment and cutting back on energy growth in the same calendar year are a few suicidal examples of this instability. A business would be foolish not to proceed with caution before expanding.

Summary

We want our country back, and turning the entrepreneurs loose will make it happen sooner rather than later. By now we should recognize that the current White House doesn't have a clue about how to solve today's economic situation. Spending our way out of the problem is only getting us in deeper. Their lack of business experience should be very obvious to everyone by now.

There is a school of thought that says the White House is intentionally deflating the economy to prepare the country for their ultimate transfer of wealth plan. Sounds preposterous—why would anyone undertake such a draconian effort? Well, why would anyone have a staff comprised of numerous avowed radicals and socialists?

My concern is that it is not an "either/or situation," but the possibility that both of the above paragraphs are accurate. I know the points in the first paragraph are accurate; I am very concerned about the items in the second one. However, if President Obama thinks he can outsmart the American public just because he has half a dozen Harvard grads on his staff, he is going to be in for a big surprise.

We won two world wars, won the Cold War, and kept the world relatively peaceful for sixty years. My military service was during a time of peace. I always regretted I did not have an opportunity to fight for my country. The fight we are involved in now is with our government. I assume during the next few years the fight for our freedom will be intense—a fight not with guns or bombs, but with words and concepts. I will not miss this fight. I intend to make up for missing the last few and putting my full force and effort to keep the government out of our businesses. Let them monitor the playing field, but don't let them try to play in it. In the process I believe we can regain many of our freedoms.

I hope you join me (and John Kennedy and Ronald Reagan) in this important effort.

CHAPTER 5

★★★★★★★★★★★★★★★★★★★★★★★★

SAVING IMMIGRATION

Population growth requires immigration.
Our culture needs to assimilate them.
Our economy and security
Are dependent on border control.

The most unique country in the world, without a doubt, is America, which was built by immigrants from virtually everywhere. These venturesome people came to our shores from faraway places like England, Germany, Italy, and Ireland—carrying with them a dream, a work ethic, and not much more. Each nationality was bound together by a common language and the hope of a better life. In the earliest days, they were bound by the goal of building a new country. Throughout America's history, our immigration policy has changed and evolved. As a country we have dramatically increased the number of people we welcome across our borders.

Certainly, people have entered America under our recognized immigration policy, but we all know that in the centuries we have been a nation, legions of people have also entered the country illegally. It is not immigration, but rather *illegal* immigration that threatens to disrupt our current policy. More importantly, left uncorrected, it will threaten the very existence of our nation.

With the help of attorney Ben Aguilera of Aguilera & Associates, I lay out a plan in this chapter that will solve our many immigration problems. You'll learn about them, too. But let me warn you. This is not an all-or-nothing plan, because when you are dealing with human lives, solutions cannot be that black and white. There are things about this plan you will like and things you won't like, no matter where you stand on the issue. But rest assured, while it may not please you in every way, it will solve our illegal immigration problems, and that should please all of us as citizens in a big way.

A Quick Look at Immigration and How We Got Here

If you're like me, at some point during the national debate on immigration, you may have wondered how things got this messed up. It certainly didn't seem like we had a problem with illegal immigration before. Or at least if we did, it wasn't this bad.

One of the reasons we're in the situation we are in is because in 1965, the Immigration and Nationality Act amendments effectively eliminated quotas on large segments of the immigration flow. As a result, legal immigration to the U.S. surged. It is estimated that between the 1950s and the 1990s the U.S. legal immigrant population skyrocketed from about 2.5 million to about 10 million. Let's fast forward to the twenty-first century. According to a *Washington Post* article written by Stephen Ohlemacher, the number of immigrants in 2006 totaled 37.5 million. The Annual Flow Report, released by the Office of Immigration Statistics in 2008, noted that a record 1,046,539 persons were naturalized as U.S. citizens. Many were "change of status" immigrants already living and working in this country, but nonetheless the number is large.

Certainly this huge influx of new residents from different cultures presents some challenges; but America is a country built on immigration, and we have been able to blend different cultures into our own quite well—albeit with a few bumps here and there, if we want to be honest about it. But overall, many, if not most, Americans appreciate their own roots and love this country at the same time. Beyond that, we've been energized by our immigrants. New Americans have a long and illustrious history of contributions to this country. That will no doubt continue.

Now let's look at *illegal* immigration. Just as legal immigration soared during the past decades, so did illegal immigration. It has been steadily climbing, with a minor downturn in 2008 largely due to the high unemployment rate in the U.S. during the recession. *Time* magazine, in a telling investigative piece titled "America's Border," reports that total illegal immigration may have been as high as three million people each year before the recession of 2008. These annual numbers are added to the estimated 12 million who are already here.

Understandably, no one knows for sure how many illegal immigrants are in the country, I have seen numbers as high as 22.5 million, and it could be even more. The point is, for as much as our *legal* immigration exploded in the last several years, it pales in comparison to the illegal aliens who call America home—at least while they are here. And all these illegal aliens are putting a strain on our systems and programs.

The Latest Invasion

It seems like we had a few good years following World War II, and then after that, the U.S. has always been at war with someone. But in only four specific instances have the American people really had any concern about being invaded. The first was in 1962 during the Cuban Missile Crisis, when we discovered Soviet missile installations just ninety miles off the coast of Florida in Cuba. I was twenty-six at the time, and it was somewhat terrifying.

The missiles were discovered on October 15, 1962, and President Kennedy announced it to the American people on October 22. Kennedy quarantined the island with a naval blockade aimed at stopping any more Soviet armaments from arriving in Cuba. He also proclaimed that any missile launched from Cuba would be considered an attack against the United States by the Soviet Union. The standoff escalated to military readiness DEFCON 3, but thankfully it lasted only a few intense days. It ended with an agreement that if the Soviets removed the missiles, the U.S. would not invade Cuba. The US returned to DEFCON 5, and the world breathed a sigh of relief. I have often wondered what would have happened if some of our other presidents were in office at the time of this crisis. I think President Kennedy did an outstanding job, and earned every dime he was ever paid.

The second time the country was concerned about an invasion was during the "Cold War," when the U.S. and Soviet Union entered the nuclear arms race. Our differences started after World War II, when—although we were allies during the war itself—the Americans and the Soviets could not agree on how to organize the post-war world. As a result, the Soviet Union formed the Eastern Bloc, and thus began the "Them vs. Us" scenario. Everything from the race-to-space propaganda that fueled rocket and missile development to the creation of enough nuclear warheads to blow up the Earth several times over happened during this forty-year period. It was a time where, despite what was going on in the front of your mind, the threat of nuclear dominance and nuclear war were constants in the back of it. The Cold War lasted until, fortunately, President Ronald Reagan put an end to it. The ultimate symbol of the end was the tearing down of the Berlin Wall, which separated the Western world from the Eastern world. Many feel that President Reagan solved the problem by forcing the Soviet Union to spend themselves into demise. Reagan, like Kennedy, also earned his pay.

The third time we felt invasion was imminent was during and after September 11, 2001, when terrorists used commercial airliners to kill thousands of people in New York, Washington, D.C., and Pennsylvania. In fact, an invasion wasn't imminent; it actually happened, but we all were fearful that it would happen again and again. The days immediately following 9/11 were like no other days most of us have ever experienced. They made us question the security we once took for granted—actually, that we never even considered—and they made us brutally aware of our place in the world. During 9/11, I was working on my first book, *Seize the American Dream: 10 Entrepreneurial Success Strategies*. I never imagined the title of that book would become such a heartfelt, powerful directive in the months and years that followed.

The fourth time we have worried about invasion is right now, and, once again, our worries are justified. It is happening as I write and you read this book. It is happening day in and day out, and despite our efforts to deter the invasion, we are not winning. Hordes of illegal aliens enter our country, and because they are undocumented, overstay their visas or commit outright visa fraud. They come, they stay, and we do very little to stop it. These people enter our country with a completely different attitude than the immigrants of past generations, who came to America to begin a better life. True, some may share the same aspirations, particularly the legal immigrants that come here and become U.S. citizens.

But illegal aliens seem to have a mission to come here, make money, send it home, and eventually go back there—wherever "there" is—and enjoy a better life for themselves and their families. I believe they are from a different mold than the immigrants of yesteryear. These people initially disrespect our border laws, and then move on to use our health care and education systems, scam our public welfare and social security systems whenever possible, and generally disrespect our laws with no intention of becoming part of America. While I have no hard data to back up my opinion, the fact that I live in Arizona, I stay informed, and for decades have heard many anecdotal stories, is all the evidence I need to help me form my opinion.

There is no doubt in my mind that our immigration laws and our country are under attack. If we as a nation do not gain control of our borders and solve the illegal immigration issue, we will be overcome from within. Most of our states are being adversely impacted by the unfunded mandates made by our national government. These are laws passed at the federal level, but not funded there. That little detail becomes the state's problem ... by law. These laws are burying states. If we now add the burden of paying for illegal aliens and all the public services a citizenry requires, every state will head down the same path as California: overwhelmed by the cost of entitlements and lawlessness, and unable to achieve any political direction that will lead to a positive outcome. It's no surprise that California is the state in the most trouble; it is also the state with the highest number of illegal aliens, by a long shot. But the numbers get worse, particularly when we talk about crime.

Illegal Aliens and Crime

It didn't take much research to uncover significant evidence that illegal aliens are involved in an inordinate number of arrests. Of course, being in this country illegally is a crime in itself. Steven Camorata, director of research for the Center for Immigration Studies, noted in 2004 that 17 percent of the federal prison population was illegal aliens. That's a very big percentage, especially when you consider that illegal aliens account for just 3 percent of the total U.S. population. The U.S. Government Accountability Office (GAO) reports that the number is as high as 27 percent of the federal prison population.

In case you've never heard of the GAO (www.gao.gov), it is an independent, non-partisan agency that works for Congress. Their mission is, in their own words, "to provide Congress with timely information that is objective, fact-based, nonpartisan, non-ideological, fair, and balanced." In addition to estimating the percentages of illegal aliens in prison compared to the population at large, they performed a study of illegal aliens who were currently incarcerated. Here's what they found:

"In our population study of 55,322 illegal aliens, we found that they were arrested at least a total of 459,614 times, averaging about 8 arrests per illegal alien. Nearly all had more than 1 arrest. Thirty-eight percent (about 21,000) had between 2 and 5 arrests, 32 percent (about 18,000) had between 6 and 10 arrests, and 26 percent (about 15,000) had 11 or more arrests.

"Most of the arrests occurred after 1990. They were arrested for a total of about 700,000 criminal offenses, averaging about 13 offenses per illegal alien. One arrest incident may include multiple offenses, a fact that explains why there are nearly one and a half times more

offenses than arrests. Almost all of these illegal aliens were arrested for more than 1 offense. Slightly more than half of the 55,322 illegal aliens had between 2 and 10 offenses. About 45 percent of all offenses were drug or immigration offenses. About 15 percent were property-related offenses such as burglary, larceny-theft, motor vehicle theft, and property damage. About 12 percent were for violent offenses such as murder, robbery, assault, and sex-related crimes. The balance was for such other offenses as traffic violations, including driving under the influence; fraud—including forgery and counterfeiting; weapons violations; and obstruction of justice. Eighty percent of all arrests occurred in three states—California, Texas, and Arizona. Specifically, about 58 percent of all arrests occurred in California, 14 percent in Texas, and 8 percent in Arizona."

This represents a huge financial burden on our nation, individual states, and our people. The nonpartisan Urban Institute, which "publishes studies, reports, and books on timely topics worthy of public consideration," took a look at the problem in their report "Illegal Aliens in Federal, State, and Local Criminal Justice Systems." This research was funded by the U.S. Department of Justice, and they confirmed that the states are putting up a fight.

"At state and local levels, the cost of arresting, prosecuting, sentencing, and supervising criminal illegal aliens has become a major issue. Six states have filed suits to force the federal government to reimburse them for criminal justice costs associated with illegal aliens. They have argued that it is the federal government's responsibility to keep illegal aliens out of this country and to expel illegal aliens who have gained entry, and that, therefore, the federal government should offset any fiscal impacts that these illegal aliens have on lower levels of government through direct reimbursement. None of these suits has been successful."

Joe Arpaio, "America's Toughest Sheriff," is a guy people either love or hate. There's no middle ground with Arpaio. He takes a very firm stance on crime and doesn't pull any punches. In Arizona, where Joe Arpaio is the Maricopa County Sheriff, the county with the nation's fifth-largest city, Phoenix, we are told that illegal immigration leads to human smuggling and drug trafficking. It is easily apparent. We see it on the local news almost nightly. It has fostered highly organized gangs, whose members roam throughout the Southwest and the country. They are fully funded, well organized, and much more vicious than the previous generations of gangs. In his book, *Criminal Alien Nation*, Edwin Rubenstein sites that criminal illegal aliens are a growing threat:

> *"In 1980, our federal and state facilities held fewer than 9,000 criminal aliens, but at the end of 2003, approximately 267,000 illegal aliens were incarcerated in U.S. correctional facilities."*

Furthermore, a January 2004 article in the *Washington Times* entitled "Illegal Criminal Aliens Abound in U.S." by Jerry Seper notes:

> *"About 80,000 illegal criminal aliens, including convicted murderers, rapists, drug dealers and child molesters who served prison time and were released, are loose on the streets of America hiding from immigration authorities."*

These facts are startling. With approximately 12 million illegal aliens living in the U.S. right now, and with these kinds of realities staring us in the face, immigration reform is a very big issue. Not necessarily because we should be afraid that a crime may be committed against us, although I suppose it is possible, but because our country and individual states cannot continue to support and fund this kind of system.

Illegal Immigration and Sanctuary Cities

You would think every major city in America would want to be tough on illegal immigration, given the facts presented so far in this chapter. But today, many cities have chosen to become "Sanctuary Cities." These are large (and a few small) urban cities that, despite the 1996

Illegal Immigration Reform and Immigrant Responsibility Act (IIRIRA) requiring local governments to work with the Department of Homeland Security's Immigration and Customs Enforcement (ICE) by notifying the federal government of any illegal aliens living within the city or town, have decided they would rather not comply and have adopted what are now called "sanctuary policies." Each city's policies are a bit different, but in essence a sanctuary policy instructs local government employees to *not* report the presence of illegal aliens in the city or town, thus blurring the lines between legal and illegal, particularly when it comes to benefitting from city services.

In Sanctuary Cities, the decision to not cooperate with immigration law is made by local politicians. And here we thought decisions that foolish could only be made in Washington! Nope. Politicians in Los Angeles, San Francisco, Chicago, New York, Houston, and others listed in this chapter are choosing to make their cities magnets for illegal aliens, both the kind coming here with good intentions and unfortunately also the ones here who will inevitably commit crimes.

Partial List of Sanctuary Cities in the U.S.

It was next to impossible to find a list that contained every Sanctuary City, because there are many opinions and lists are continually under review based on city policies and behaviors. For a more complete list visit www.ojjpac.org/sanctuary.asp.

Anchorage, AK	Cicero, IL	Aztec, NM
Fairbanks, AK	Cambridge, MA	Rio Arriba, County, NM
Chandler, AZ	Orleans, MA	Santa Fe, NM
Phoenix, AZ	Portland, ME	New York, NY
Fresno, CA	Baltimore, MD	Ashland, OR
Los Angeles, CA	Takoma Park, MD	Gaston, OR
National City, CA	Ann Arbor, MI	Marion County, OR
San Diego, CA	Detroit, MI	Austin, TX
San Francisco, CA	Minneapolis, MN	Houston, TX
Sonoma County, CA	Newark, NJ	Katy, TX
New Haven, CT	Trenton, NJ	Virginia Beach, VA
Evanston, IL	Durham, NC	Seattle, WA
Chicago, IL	Albuquerque, NM	Madison, WI

Please, someone, tell me, when I or a family member gets mugged by an illegal alien and suffers injuries, who in the local government should I name in the case? The mayor? Yeah, why not? Make it the mayor, not the council, not the city, but the mayor, personally. It is too bad you can't sue someone for just pure ignorance. Sanctuary Cities, you are not helping the illegal immigration problem. You are the problem, or least a big part of it. As long as there are havens, there will be illegal aliens.

Illegal Aliens and Multiculturalism

As I stated at the beginning of this chapter, early immigrants came to this country for a new beginning, intent on becoming a part of a new country. Qualification for citizenship was not available until they could speak English, and knew some American history facts. Over time, after some rocky starts, the immigrants of yesterday became enveloped in the American culture and way of life and thought of their original homeland not as home, but as "The Old Country." That said it all. Yesterday's immigrants became Americans.

Today's immigrants, particularly illegal aliens, are less interested in integrating into the American way of life. They are more interested in maintaining their Old Country's culture and have a tendency to stay around or within an area populated by their former nationality and be educated in their own language. Consequently, instead of building one country—the true melting pot for which America is famous—we see ourselves faced with a multicultural country.

We are not alone. Australia, Canada, France, Spain, England, and Holland are having significant problems of their own. Certainly with our legal immigrants we have a chance to redirect some of the cultural efforts to build one country. With the illegal aliens we have no chance.

I liked what President Teddy Roosevelt had to say about the subject of immigration. Perhaps it can help us shape our own attitudes. These are his words, from 1907:

"In the first place, we should insist that if the immigrant who comes here in good faith becomes an American and assimilates himself to us, he shall be treated on an exact equality with everyone else for it is an outrage to discriminate against any such man because of creed, or birthplace, or origin. But this is predicated upon the person's becoming in every facet an American, and nothing but an American. There can be no divided allegiance here. Any man who says he is an American, but something else also, isn't an American at all. We have room for but one flag, the American flag. We have room for but one language here, and that is the English language. And we have room for but one sole loyalty and that is a loyalty to the American people."

Teddy was right then, and he is right now! We are still the melting pot, but we want one pot, not several. This is our country, and those of us who are citizens want it run in a manner that will prove successful and lead us towards one integrated culture. We recognize that our politicians have taken us down the wrong road during the last few decades, but that doesn't mean it cannot be corrected.

Illegal Aliens and Health Care

According to the Emergency Medical Treatment and Active Labor Act of 1985 (EMTALA), hospitals in America must provide emergency medical treatment to any person who walks into an emergency room. This means those who are uninsured, those who are not U.S. citizens, and those who cannot pay must be treated by law. I understand the moral obligation, but what I don't understand is that while the government mandates the hospitals to care for these patients, it offers no form of reimbursement for the services. In essence, the work is done for free.

In cities or towns where this kind of humanitarian work occasionally happens, it's no problem. But what about in cities where emergency rooms are flooded with illegal aliens who came to this country not for a better life, but simply for free medical care? The Johns

Hopkins University's *Hopkins Undergraduate Research Journal's* article "The Effect of Illegal Immigration on the U.S. Healthcare System" clearly states that illegal aliens in some parts of the country have abused the system to the point of system breakdown. The author, Mehdi Draoua, states:

> *"...between 1993 and present day, over 60 hospitals have closed down in the state of California due to the surge in critical care given to those without insurance, mainly illegal immigrants. While some may blame this simply on business fluctuations, since hospitals are usually run by private firms, one cannot deny a problem in the system when many of these closed hospitals reported no payment for over 50% of their services."*

Can you see just how big a problem illegal immigration is, and how little is really being done about it? It seems like we are in continual discussion and debate mode, building fences that don't work, surveillance systems that don't work, adding bigger guns to too few border patrol men and women. Meanwhile, we're not taking care of the 12-million-person problem we have currently in our cities.

The Solutions

I think by now I have made my case, and you comprehend the scale of the problem and what is at stake. Now it's time for some solutions. As you may realize by now, I take an entrepreneurial approach. Think of it as a new policy: Entrepreneurial Control of Immigration and Illegal Immigration.

Border Control

Until we as a people insist we have strong border control, our future as a country will be in danger. We are being invaded by hordes of illegal immigrants from Latin America, which include criminals and terrorists. This first line of defense is so necessary and so obvious, it is hard to understand why it has not been a national priority. We have soldiers all over the world guarding borders; how about having them protect us first? This seems so basic ... I can't believe I even have to point it out.

Employer Sanctions

We need to enforce the current law, which says hiring illegal immigrants is a crime. Having a law and not enforcing it is senseless. I understand that much of America has been built on the backs of illegal alien labor, but thanks to greed, speculation, and now a drain on services and a reduced tax base due to the recession, there's not much being built at all. The time is now to get our business models in place so that appropriate labor can fuel the next growth cycle. Businesses need to do the right thing not just for themselves, but for our nation. Otherwise America won't be saved.

Sanctuary Designations

Okay, let's eliminate this immediately. Local police must uphold the law and cooperate by reporting illegal aliens within their jurisdictions. And they must have the cooperation of federal officials in all matters of illegal immigration. I thought one of the purposes of Homeland Security was to coordinate all the law enforcement agencies. The last big mandate I remember from this government department was a Code Orange airport alert, and once they told us to buy plastic and duct tape to seal off our homes from a potential biological weapons threat. Good idea ... that would work. It's time they start earning their pay.

Language

Language unites. It's as simple as that. English should be the official language in all states, including California. One nation, one language.

Eligibility

My friend and colleague, attorney Ben Aguilera, provided these qualification requirements for this book. He believes that by ignoring the creation of a comprehensive program, we are "punting on an issue that has strong economic repercussions as well as strong national security consequences." Amen to that. Here are his criteria:

1. Only applicants in good standing should qualify. (In other words, without a criminal record, not on a terrorist watch list, and without a serious misdemeanor such as an extreme DUI.)

2. Illegal aliens who have been in the country for at least five years and who are in good standing prior to their application would be granted permanent residency status, *not* immediate citizenship. After five or more years under a permanent residency status, they should be allowed to apply for citizenship if they have remained in good standing (i.e. without any of the circumstances mentioned above).

3. Applicants for permanent residency status under the program do not have to leave the U.S. to apply for such adjusted status. Rather, they could travel to one of sixteen ports of entry, where they could file for that adjustment.

4. Institute a temporary worker program that would allow numerous entries and exits. Specifically, targeted industries or positions should be open to undocumented men and women currently employed in the U.S., as well as to new foreign workers.

5. American workers will be preferred. Employers must make every reasonable effort to find an American to fill a job before extending job offers to undocumented men and women currently living in the U.S., or to foreign workers.

6. Illegal immigrants who have been in the country for less than five years prior to filing their application should receive consideration under the free guest worker program and need not leave the U.S. to apply for such adjusted status. Rather, they

should travel to one of sixteen ports of entry, where they could file for such adjustment.

7. All guest workers would have the opportunity to apply for permanent residency and later for citizenship.

8. Guest workers would be allowed to remain in the country for six years, and during the fourth year, if they are in good standing, they could apply for permanent residency status. After five years as permanent residents, the former guest workers, if they are in good standing, should be allowed to apply for citizenship.

Summary

Illegal immigration is destroying our country. It brings with it crime, drugs, human smuggling, and misuse of our health care and welfare systems. Our number-one issue or problem is lack of border control. Any proposed solution without strong border control will be worthless and near impossible to enact. Our country is a country of *legal* immigrants. Illegal immigrants will tear it down faster than it was ever built. Not only is that devastating to future generations, but it shows complete disrespect and dishonor for generations of fathers and mothers who, as immigrants to America, built this country and made it great. They and their legacy deserve much better than we as a nation are giving them.

★★★★★★★★★★★★★★★★★★★★★★★★★★★★

CHAPTER 6

SAVING CONGRESS

Congress needs to lead
The entire free world
With unquestionable ethics
And intellectual debate.

About thirty years ago, my wife and I visited the U.S. Capitol while the Senate was in session. Normally, you sit in a designated area for about twelve minutes before they cycle in a new batch of tourists. My wife and I sat someplace else, not because we were trying to shirk the system, but because we wanted better seats. I guess that's why we were never asked to leave. We sat in the Senate chamber for an hour and a half, and the show was amazing. It wasn't one guy talking to a television camera like you see today on C-SPAN. Just about every senator you'd ever heard of was in that chamber, and they were engaged in a lively, intelligent debate on the investment tax credit, a bill similar to one I think could have merit today.

I'll never forget the late Senator Ted Kennedy's speech. He praised the Republican who had spoken before him, calling him a good person, a family man, and a fine addition to the Senate. Then he proceeded to rip that Republican apart because of his stance on tax credits. I remember thinking this was something of which to be proud. As long as we had a body of government engaged in such healthy and productive debate, it didn't matter who was in the White House. No legislation was going to get through this place unless it was good for the American people.

If you need a minute to control your laughter, I understand. It's probably been a while since you heard anyone describe the Senate in such glowing terms. As of Christmas 2009, Americans' approval rating of Congress stood at a pathetic 25 percent in a *USA Today*/Gallup poll. It's no wonder. What once was a beacon of hope, a bastion of honor, and a body of debate and compromise has devolved into a savvy stable of self-serving elitists. There is no honor left in the Senate. There is no shame. There is no discernible service to the constituents, and there is little concern for the future of our great nation.

The Senate has forfeited most of its power and authority to the White House, rendering it a largely irrelevant body. Its lack of concern for the future of our nation has allowed our annual deficit and our national debt to rise to unprecedented levels. And the Senate's willingness, even eagerness, to accept campaign donations from lobbyists has transformed it into a den of thieves.

There is only one solution to this problem: Vote every incumbent out of office and start from scratch. Republicans and Democrats alike have put our country on a perilous road to financial ruin. This chapter will retrace the missteps and reveal the congressional changes we must make to save Congress, or should I say, save Congress from itself.

Misstep #1: Broken Promises

When President George W. Bush signed No Child Left Behind (NCLB) into law in 2002, the goals were laudable: Create and enforce higher national education standards, and ensure that the needs of disadvantaged and at-risk groups were being met by 2016. As is often the case with government programs, the implementation tripped up the idea.

While the federal government appropriated billions of dollars for NCLB, a large number of states received less than what they were promised, and less than what they needed to properly implement the program. Ohio, for example, says it spends about $1.5 billion each year to implement the law—much more than it gets from the federal government. Between fiscal years 2003 and 2008, the cumulative gap between what federal lawmakers authorized to be used for NCLB and what they actually appropriated, nationwide, was $40.5 billion. If the political will existed to create NCLB, why doesn't the political will exist to fund it?

Under NCLB, federal funding is tied to a school district's achievement levels, including the test scores of at-risk groups, such as lower-income families and English-as-a-second-language students. To ensure these at-risk populations are achieving the new standards requires additional money. Why? For starters, students in impoverished areas often need tutoring, and districts often need community outreach programs to offset the indifference to education found in many lower-income families. If you're going to improve the performance of lower-income students, you have to change the culture. That costs money.

As you just learned, the states aren't getting that money from Congress. This is called an unfunded mandate, and the federal government is notorious for this sort of legislation. Pass a law and then leave it to the states and taxpayers to figure out how to pay for it. That's lousy leadership. States are cash-strapped already because of the slumping economy. They don't have the money to pay their teachers a decent wage, let alone pay for additional testing, more teachers, after-school classes, summer school, tutoring, and community outreach programs—all necessities if the districts are to meet the requirements of NCLB. And if the states don't meet these worthy but unrealistic goals, it's the children who suffer when what little federal funding there is gets pulled.

But wait. There's more. The 2003 Medicare prescription drug program, often referred to as the Medicare Overhaul, provided generous federal subsidies toward the purchase of prescription drugs by Medicare beneficiaries. It was supposed to drive down costs and give people more choices. It was supposed to make life simpler for seniors. Instead, it created a confusing labyrinth of choices and reimbursement policies while leaving the elderly holding the bag for a significant fraction of the bill.

After an initial deductible and co-payments, Medicare currently covers the first $2,700 in annual prescription costs. After that, seniors pay for their prescriptions out of their own pockets. This is called the coverage gap, unaffectionately referred to by seniors as the "doughnut hole," because it leaves beneficiaries on their own to cover costs until they reach $6,154 in total annual drug costs. That's when Medicare coverage kicks in again and beneficiaries only have to pay 5 percent of the bill. So seniors who incur drug costs in excess of $2,700 per year are flying without a net until they reach $6,154 in annual costs, if they ever do. But here's the other problem: the gap isn't constant. The size of the gap increases with drug costs, so it grows faster than the incomes of most seniors every year.

Here's another, unrelated surprise that came with the Medicare overhaul: payments to private Medicare Advantage plans. These are payments that have been, on average, 14 percent higher for Medicare beneficiaries than if they had just stayed with traditional Medicare. Now Congress is on the cusp of passing a massive health care reform bill with an estimated price tag of $1 trillion. It's another promise of affordable health care for all Americans. Anyone want to guess what the real costs will be when all is said and done? Anyone want to guess how efficient this comprehensive new plan will be? Anyone want to guess who's going to get stuck with the unexpected costs? Us!

So, here's what happens: Congress makes laws, passes them, and then leaves it up to the states to fund them. Those "unfunded mandates" have to stop. That's congressional change #1.

Speaking of broken promises, how about that federal stimulus package and the so-called Troubled Asset Relief Program loans? I believe TARP was a good idea at its inception. We couldn't let our banks fail or our entire economic system would have crumbled. However, the original plan was for the banks to repay their loans—which many have done—and to apply those payments to the debt. Now President Obama and Congress are mulling using those payments for other purposes. Sorry America, we're breaking our promises to you again.

Misstep #2: Earmarks

When Dwight D. Eisenhower was president, there was probably an average of six earmarks per congressional bill. Now there are sixty, or maybe 600. Who knows? The public never sees them anyway. It's like a bottomless grab-bag where every member of Congress gets a present and every taxpayer picks up the tab. In fiscal year 2008, the total worth of congressional earmarks was $18.3 billion. The math worked like this: 11,234 earmarks worth $14.8 billion and another $3.5 billion where no sponsoring member of Congress was identified. That's a whopping number of under-the-table deals.

Now, I don't think all earmarks are bad. I think we can all agree that earmarks funding autism or cancer research are worthy dollars spent. On the other hand, Alaska Sen. Ted Stevens' infamous bridge to nowhere was ridiculous. Not that anyone in the Senate told him so. The argument you always hear regarding earmarks is, "This is how things get done in Washington." Well, in my eyes, Washington needs a new system. These people are supposed to be leaders, not people who are afraid to call a halt to a bad spend for fear their own unworthy pet project might get the ax, too. That's not leadership, that's simply self-serving.

At the risk of sounding obvious, if that's the way things are done in Washington, then something is terribly wrong. What senators regularly do to obtain votes for the passage of legislation (buy other senators' votes) and what they regularly categorize as earmarks would put most businessmen in jail. I'm sure America's taxpayers could dream up far more creative punishments for the beloved Senate.

The federal stimulus package is a classic example of earmarks gone awry. Aside from the debate over whether the package has actually created jobs—the White House says it has, Republicans say it hasn't—the final version of the bill was packed full of pork. Here's a list of some of the more self-serving, or outright bizarre, earmarks that worked their way into the stimulus:

- $198 million to compensate Filipino World War II veterans, most of whom don't live in the United States, for their service. This came from Sen. Daniel Inouye, D-Hawaii.
- $50 million for habitat restoration and other water needs in the San Francisco Bay Area.
- $2 million to train Native Americans for careers as plumbers and pipefitters.
- An insurance exemption, but only for companies that work on recreational boats longer than 65 feet. (Are you kidding me?)
- $62 million for military projects in Guam. Yes, I said Guam.

Now that you've read these, I think you'll agree we need to limit earmarks. How we determine what's worthy of an earmark and what's not should be debated, if that is still possible in the current political climate. Regardless, the process is clearly crying out for limits, unless we're okay with making Alaska the bridge capital of the world.

So here's congressional change #2: If we're going to have earmarks, we need to trumpet their contents from the mountaintops. Don't let Congress get away with business as usual. Don't let the ship sail into port and unload its cargo without first inspecting that cargo. And don't let one state pass the cost of its Christmas wish list on to the rest of the nation. I heard California Governor Arnold Schwarzenegger giving a speech the other day that made me laugh. He said, "[Nebraska] got the corn. We got the husk." He was referring to the outrageous Medicaid funding exemption Nebraska got for voting in favor of the health care bill. Our elected officials should go back to Washington and say, "We don't want this health care bill unless we get the same deal as Nebraska. And we certainly shouldn't have to foot the bill for Nebraska."

Misstep #3: Campaign Contributions

The greatest hurdle to Congress performing its job admirably is that evil little critter known as the campaign contribution, or should I say "bribe." There are hundreds of lobbyists telling senators and representatives, "If you take care of me on this bill, I'll make a $50,000 donation to your campaign." If a senator runs four, five, or six campaigns in his or her lifetime, and if he or she is frugal, those dollars can really add up. They get so big, in fact, that it takes an unusual man or woman to resist them.

Like earmarks, I don't think all lobbyists are evil. Some lobbyists are vital to the democratic process. It's impossible for Congress to be aware of, and educated on, every issue under the sun. There's just too much information out there. Lobbyists provide an avenue to enlightenment, enabling our lawmakers to make more informed decisions. But if you sleep with dogs, you'll eventually wake up with fleas, and that's what happens when money gets involved. That's why ethics has become a major issue in Congress.

Think about it. Let's say I run a construction business and I want a company to choose my bid for a big job. Suppose I make a big contribution to that company's pension fund. I don't care how many hairs you split, that's a bribe. As soon as a lobbyist pays a senator in the form of a campaign donation, that's a bribe. And when the senator has the gall to say that's the way things get done, that statement is as offensive to the American people as is the original bribe. Wrong is wrong, no matter how long we've been accepting it.

Ready for congressional change #3? We need to eliminate pay to play. We need to eliminate the financial influence of lobbyists. This is no easy task, of course. We all know how well those efforts have gone in the past. Remember the Bipartisan Campaign Reform Act (BCRA), also called the McCain-Feingold bill after its chief sponsors, senators John McCain and Russ Feingold? It eliminated all soft-money donations to the national party committees, but in doing so, it also doubled the contribution limit of hard money per election cycle. Nobody in

Washington is truly interested in curbing these donations. The pay-offs are just too enticing.

The plain and simple truth is this: If you don't have money, you don't have influence with or access to Congress. I laugh when I hear people say, "Oh, you need to get involved. You need to call your senator." Well, go ahead. Call your senator and see what happens. You'll get transferred to his voicemail, and then you'll get a message telling you his voicemail is full. There's no access. Of course, they don't have any problem calling you three to four times a quarter to ask you for money, but when you try to call them and obtain information, you're ignored.

And speaking of those campaign donations, what happens to them when a member of Congress leaves office? I know there are strict laws regarding the use of campaign contributions. None can be used to increase personal wealth, but the laws are not as strict as they should be, otherwise Al Gore wouldn't have steered funds to key players in his pet crusade, global warming. All campaign contributions should go back to the taxpayers, not to political parties, their causes, or the next wave of candidates.

Misstep #4: Misrepresentation

I believe that neo-conservatives who think like Rush Limbaugh and Sean Hannity have a greater representation in Congress than they do in our society at large. I think the same is true for the ultra-liberals. Somehow, the people who represent us are more polarized in their views than the general population, and they have far too much control over party platforms and messages. We've never been so divided as a nation. Each side spends most of its day screaming at the other, and these extremists only fan the flames.

Part of the problem stems from the constant redrawing of district boundaries. Since lawmakers are allowed to redraw congressional districts at the federal and state levels, they do it and each year, and those districts become more politically polarized. You don't see many districts whose constituents are a nice blend of Republicans and Democrats like you saw back in the 1950s. They're either one or the other, and the message of the representative reflects that growing polarization.

Congressional change #4 is simply this: Please, represent us *all*, not just the polarized left and right. We need to return to a time of civil debate and meaningful compromise. We need more moderate voices that accurately reflect America as a whole. In the long term, I think we might need a viable third party to force coalition-building and civil discourse to shake the existing parties out of their comfort zone. But in the short term, there's no doubt we need to diffuse the Democratic control of Congress and the White House. If we don't save Congress from Democratic control—if we let President Obama do what he wants for the next two or three years—our country will be so damaged by the time we reach another election that we may not be able to recover.

I think a certain percentage of people will vote Republican or Democrat no matter what the candidates are saying, but if we can get to the point where the Democrats at least have to talk to Republicans to get bills passed (and vice versa), we might achieve some form of sensibility. If you have equal numbers of members on either side of the aisle, you have to compromise and form coalitions.

In the long run, I hope the emergence of the Tea Parties sparks a political revolution in America, and the forming of a third party. What I hope comes out of the Tea Parties in the short term is that we get some of the big spenders, Republicans and Democrats, out of Congress, and get others in. For the Tea Parties to succeed long term, they can't be associated with either existing party. We're already seeing efforts by the Republicans to hijack and compromise these Tea Parties. The Senate is full of fat cats, who are mostly bent on increasing their own wealth. It is the most egregious example of what's wrong. This current Senate is not the one our founding fathers imagined. We need to take back America. We might as well start with the Senate.

Summary

Congress is overdue for a massive overhaul. There's no point in beating around the bush. They spend too much, yield to special interests, are unwilling to compromise, and in general play to their own personal agenda. Last time I checked, that was not the definition of a leader or a statesman. To save America, we must save Congress. These fair congressional changes are what it will take.

Be certain that when we pass federal legislation, we can also fund that legislation. No more unfunded mandates! Limit earmarks that benefit one state at the expense of the nation's taxpayers. Remove the influence of lobbyist money in the form of campaign contributions. The practice is unseemly, unlawful, and it undermines the democratic process. Restore a climate of civil debate and meaningful compromise. The neo-conservatives and ultra-liberals have hijacked the party platforms and messages. We need to take them back. That may mean we need a third party.

It may happen if we vote all incumbents out. Regardless of how we do it, this nation needs congressional change. No real reform is possible in this country unless this happens.

Now you understand my plan to achieve this reform. When it's time to vote, vote for congressional change!

CHAPTER 7

SAVING THE MILITARY

The military veterans
Are never thanked enough.
We can never forget
Their years of sacrifice.

Over the course of my life, which included two years in the United States Army at Fort Sill, Oklahoma, I have met and spoken with a number of men and women who served our country in times of war. Whether it was the man I mentioned in the dedication of this book who fought on Iwo Jima, or some other soldier, all have shared their memories with me, hoping to convey that unforgettable experience. The stories are spellbinding—filled with horror, death, humor, and bravery. But no account or explanation can substitute for the real thing. War is truly a "you-had-to-be-there" event.

I was one of the lucky ones. I served in the Army during peacetime. I've often felt a tinge of guilt when I encounter these brave veterans who put their lives on the line to fight for a country they love. We have come a long way toward honoring veterans in the United States. Cries of "support the troops" have replaced the unthinkable epithets of "baby killer" that were shouted at Vietnam veterans as they returned home after years in the cruel and deadly jungles of Southeast Asia.

Recent research tells us that veteran benefits like health care have improved dramatically over the years thanks to the efforts of Presidents Bill Clinton and George W. Bush, Sen. Bob Dole, and a number of others. But we can and should do more. If one veteran goes without the care he or she deserves, that is one too many. If one veteran cannot find a job when he or she is qualified, that is one too many.

And if one veteran feels the sting of disenfranchisement when returning home, we must help that man or woman find the way.

Recent abuses by American military personnel at detention facilities around the world have created an outcry for more oversight and punishment. I believe strongly that those who break the laws and codes of the armed forces should be brought to justice. But the misdeeds of a few should not overshadow the bravery and sacrifice of thousands. And they must not deter us from our mission.

We need a strong military because our enemies are real—whether they reside in the remote mountains of Pakistan, the hardened streets of Mexico, or the sweltering deserts of Iraq. We need a strong military to protect our economic and political interests around the world.

But we also need a stronger support system for our military when it is time for them to return to civilian life. The men and women who serve are heroes. It is their sacrifice upon which this nation was built. It is their sacrifice by which this nation will be protected. And it is their sacrifice upon which this nation will grow and prosper.

Some Perspective

This section will provide some perspective, and in subsequent sections, we'll cover the problems, and pose solutions. As I mentioned earlier, the horrors of war cannot effectively be conveyed through words or images. Yet it is still important to read and re-read accounts of war to comprehend just how much was gained and how much was lost. It is important to watch films like *Saving Private Ryan* or the wonderful HBO series *Band of Brothers* to see the suffering our troops endured in the cause of freedom. It is important to visit the war memorials and cemeteries here in the United States and in France, where you can gaze at crosses stretching all the way to the horizon, and understand the scale of death suffered in conflict.

The table on the next page is a small attempt to do just that. In some ways, the numbers are mind-numbing in their scope. It's hard to fathom the 416,800 American military personnel who died during World War II until you consider that's roughly the population of modern-day Miami. It's hard to imagine the nearly 26,000 Americans who died during the Meuse-Argonne Offensive in World War I until you think, "That's like wiping out the entire student population at the University of Kansas."

Some of the death figures vary, depending on the source, but that variance does not diminish the sobering reality. I urge you to browse through the figures and gain your own perspective. I hope it colors

---

Sobering Statistics: American Wars of the Past 150 Years

Deaths From Battles:

- Civil War (1861–65): 618,222 dead*
- World War I (1917–18): 116,708 dead*
- World War II (1941–45): 416,800 dead*
- Korean War (1950–53): 54,246 dead†
- Vietnam War (1965–73): 58,220 dead†
- Persian Gulf War (1990–91): 1,947 dead†
- Operation Enduring Freedom/Afghanistan (2001–present): 936 dead†
- Operation Iraqi Freedom (2003–present): 4,361 dead†

Casualties From Battles:

- The Battle of Gettysburg, Civil War (July 1–3, 1863): 51,112 dead*
- The Meuse-Argonne Offensive, World War I (Sept. 26–Nov. 11, 1918): 26,000 dead‡
- The Battle of the Bulge, World War II (Dec. 16, 1944–Jan. 25, 1945): 19,246 dead‡
- The Battle of Iwo Jima, World War II (Feb. 19, 1945): 6,821 dead*
- The Battle of Chosin Reservoir, Korean War (Nov. 27–Dec. 13, 1950): 1,029 dead*
- Tet Offensive, Vietnam War (Jan. 31–Feb. 24, 1968): 1,536 dead*

* Source: U.S. National Archives
† Source: U.S. Department of Defense
‡ Source: United States Department of the Army

your opinion when reading the rest of this chapter.

The men and women of the military deserve the best we have to offer. This is what I propose we do for them.

Proposal #1: Reform Veterans' Health Care

When a man or woman returns from war, he or she comes back changed. Sometimes the changes are physical, but they are *always* emotional. No matter how well you can bear the realities of war, you come back a different person. And sometimes, oftentimes, that person needs care. In America, care comes through the Veterans Health Administration (VHA).

The Veterans Health Administration was once a mismanaged bureaucracy of unkempt, unsafe facilities with unresponsive healthcare. Thousands of eligible patients chose other forms of care rather than put their faith in the VHA. But since the middle of the 1990s, a dramatic and largely unseen transformation has turned the VHA into a system some now consider a model. The VHA's extensive use of electronic medical records technology, its organizational restructuring designed to facilitate decision-making authority, its performance measurements targeted toward improving the quality of care, and its focus on preventive care have helped the VHA outperform Medicare and many private health plans on a number of key measures. Repeated surveys have shown that most VHA members are very satisfied with the level of care they receive.

It's not surprising, then, that demand at veterans clinics and hospitals has soared. Since 1995, the number of patients the VHA serves on an annual basis has more than doubled. In 2005, the Bush administration admitted it had underestimated the number of eligible military personnel returning from Iraq and Afghanistan, warning that the VHA's programs would fall short by at least $2.6 billion in 2006 unless Congress approved additional funds.

This continues to be the biggest source of concern with the VHA. The organization released a report in February of 2009, that said one-quarter of the 105,000 Afghanistan and Iraq veterans diagnosed with post-traumatic stress disorder had to wait more than thirty days for an appointment at any one of the VHA's 168 medical centers and 800 clinics. VHA policy states that medical staff must see veterans with serious service-related disabilities within thirty days of their requested appointment date.

Part of the problem is that some of the technology fell short—specifically the VHA's $167-million patient scheduling program, which has proved to be a complete failure despite eight years in development. Tight budgets are the other culprit, and there has been little offered in the way of substantive solutions. President Obama's quickly shelved plan to make private insurers pay for the treatment of combat injuries and other service-related health issues was insulting, and roundly criticized by most veterans groups. While it would not, as was often misreported, have required veterans to pay for health care out of their own pockets, it very likely would have raised the cost of health care for veterans and made it harder for them to find civilian jobs with employers forced to absorb the cost of service-related health issues. It was a bad move that, along with these other problems, have gotten in the way of care.

Enough of this nonsense! When men and women are willing to lay down their lives in service to their country, you don't quibble over the cost of caring for them. That cost, no matter how high, is part of the deal, and it's not open for debate. The VHA should have the required funds to provide quality care for veterans, whatever their needs. Naturally, it's important for the VHA to manage its cost through efficient operations, a goal it appears to be reaching after the aforementioned overhaul, but there is no room for talk of limiting funds or service for the nation's veterans. Let's make sure the VHA is properly funded, even if it means sacrificing elsewhere within the federal budget.

Proposal #2: Get Jobs for GI Joe & Jane

We came across a disturbing piece of information recently. It came our way courtesy of Dan Caulfield, an ex-Marine and the chairman of the board of the Hire a Hero program operated by the Armed Forces Support Foundation. Hire a Hero helps the military community network so its members can find the best career opportunities and support as they reintegrate into civilian society. During his research, Caulfield found that ex-military personnel are three to five times less likely to be hired for the same job as their civilian counterparts. Caulfield attributes this to a basic stereotype employers have about the military: that they're good at following orders and little else.

Caulfield is right when he says military personnel have a highly tuned set of job skills, whether it's effective communication, rapid decision-making, or the ability to sell a vision. I worked with many former military men at Burroughs Corporation and IBM. I hired a lot of them, too, when I ran my own businesses. As a rule, the men and women who came out of the military and worked for me were as good as, or better than, the people coming out of college—especially those who came from the officer ranks. They were sharp and they were all ready to roll up their sleeves and go to work. There is no room for laziness in the armed forces.

Fortunately, there are several online services available to ex-military men and women to make the task of finding civilian jobs a bit easier, but, as Caulfield has noted, those services can only get our servicemen and women in the door for interviews. They don't do the hiring, and they can't change the misconceptions employers have about the military. I'm not a believer in affirmative action programs, so I would not advocate incentives for businesses to hire ex-military personnel, but I'd really like to see us do a better job of educating employers about the advantages of hiring military personnel. Perhaps a massive public-relations push would be in order. Military personnel possess a bevy of job skills that take college graduates years to learn. We owe it to the men and women of our armed forces to provide a smooth financial transition back to civilian life. Their skills can only enhance our business community.

Proposal #3: Protect Our Interests the Right Way

The global reach of the U.S. military today is unprecedented. According to official Pentagon statistics, more than 190,000 troops and 115,000 civilian employees are massed in approximately 900 military facilities in forty-six countries and territories (the unofficial figure is far greater) around the world. The U.S. military owns or rents 795,000 acres of land, with 26,000 buildings and structures, valued at $146 billion. These bases provide a number of strategic benefits. They guarantee access to markets and natural resources like oil, they afford the U.S. the ability to respond quickly to crises, and they are, no doubt, an intimidating reminder of America's power.

Critics of America's global net of bases argue that any strategic gains are offset by the political, social, and environmental damage these bases create in their host nations. This argument is worth considering, but only as a means to improve our operations in foreign lands. We must be sensitive to cultural differences and public opinion in those nations, but we must never forfeit our strategic advantage. The rise of China as a global economic power will continue to pose a serious threat to American preeminence. Already, the Chinese have a greater strategic foothold in Africa because they were quick to recognize the do's and don'ts of the continent and keep their politics separate from their business dealings. We should take China's threat seriously and do whatever we can to maintain our strategic advantages.

The ever-increasing U.S. federal deficit makes maintaining our network of bases increasingly challenging. As our annual debt repayment increases and other social programs (worthy or not) eat up a greater share of the federal budget, the logical conclusion is that America's defense spending must be cut. But regardless of what Rep. Barney Frank says, I wouldn't cut it one bit. I'd make sure our soldiers have everything they need, and I'd cut the heck out of just about every other program to make it happen.

Just as with any other business, our military bases must be run efficiently from both a cost and operation standpoint. Any business operation should constantly evaluate itself to locate areas for improvement. This is already happening at our military bases. Forward Operating Locations (FOLs) are a new concept in Pentagon planning. They are smaller than conventional military bases and are designed to help fight conventional and unconventional threats abroad. In South America, for example, FOLs also serve as radar tracking sites to locate drug traffickers and terrorists. The advantages of FOLs are many-fold. They are cheaper, they are smaller and therefore easier to mobilize, and their size makes them more tolerable to civilian populations. Yet they can still be expanded quickly in times of crisis.

I also say the military must remain on the cutting edge of technology to maintain superiority over the rest of the world. At times, greater technology can save money. At other times, the cost of new equipment can be daunting to the average taxpayer, but the alternative cost is far greater: the loss of America's freedom. Technology must be at the forefront of any military planning, and I challenge the military brass on the value of technology defenses vs. boots on the ground. There is nothing that sways the court of public opinion quite like the loss of American lives, and I believe that our air superiority and other technologies can, in many cases, replace the need for infantry. But in the end, I'd go with whatever the military decided they needed. It's that important.

After all, the global economy is predicated on the safe flow of energy supplies and goods. Any interruption of that supply would have serious, negative consequences throughout the world. Given the world's current state, can we really afford an interruption of any significance? I don't think so.

Summary

If this chapter accomplished nothing else, I hope it left you with a greater sense of the sacrifice our military men and women make for this country—a sacrifice they've been making for more than two centuries. The forfeiture of life is the greatest sacrifice a person can make for a cause, and these men and women are willing to do it every day of their lives. In turn, we must do everything in our power to support them in the field and support them when they return to civilian life. We must take care of their health needs. We must find them jobs and, on a more personal note, we should thank them for protecting our interests, protecting our freedoms, and keeping us safe.

CHAPTER 8

SAVING EDUCATION

Math, science, and English
Supported by computer science.
The goal is excellence
For K-12 and college.

Brace yourself. If you haven't heard the facts about the American education system, you are about to read a few right now. The next few moments may make you angry, nervous, or just plain shocked. I don't care. The way I see it, in business you can't fix what you don't know is broken, and it takes the facts to make good decisions. When it comes to education in this country, a *lot* is broken. It's time to get down to business and fix it. Way *past* the time, actually.

The American educational system is under attack on all fronts. Parents, politicians, academia, and the media have assailed the current system as ineffective, inefficient, and unresponsive. But those are qualitative words; let's look at the statistics. A 2009 analysis by the National Center for Education Statistics (NCES) found that 15-year-old American students placed well below the average in math and science scores, compared to other participating countries. In math, U.S. high school students placed in the bottom quarter of participating countries, trailing nations like Finland, China, and Estonia. In science, the U.S. was behind countries like Canada, Japan, and the Czech Republic.

The Third International Mathematics and Science Study (TIMSS), involving a half-million students in forty-one countries, found that U.S. math and science scores steadily decline from fourth grade until twelfth grade, compared to other nations' scores. By the time our students reach the twelfth grade, their scores are near the bottom, outdistancing only the countries of Cyprus and South Africa.

The bad news doesn't stop there. Would you be surprised to learn that the math tests we demand for high school diplomas require knowledge that other countries learn in the *seventh grade*? Would you be surprised to learn that middle school students are using textbooks full of errors and inaccuracies? Would you be surprised to learn that our high school honors level textbooks are no more difficult than those an eighth grader used fifty years ago? Would you be surprised to learn that many science and math teachers have little science or math training?

It doesn't take a rocket scientist to figure out the consequences of this across-the-board decline. Students represent our future—whether they enter the business world, politics, or even teaching! If one-third of our economy depends on trade, and if the global challenges to America are accelerating on a daily basis, what happens when our workforce isn't properly trained? You do the math (if you can).

This chapter will examine how we got ourselves into this education mess, and what we need to do to fix it. I'm not concerned solely with our failings in science and math. They're just the clearest and most recognizable symbols of a system in distress—flashing neon signs that scream: Problem! There are other problems of equal weight, and there are many of them, from teacher compensation and low or non-existent standards, to misallocation of resources. The American educational system is experiencing a systemic breakdown. We need an all-hands-on-deck approach to fix it.

Unions Have Hijacked Teaching

Let me start by saying I am not anti-union. It's unfortunate we've gotten to the point where many people believe unions are bad. They are not all bad. Some of the older industries in this nation benefited from the advent of unions during the Industrial Revolution. In many cases, companies were abusing employees with unsafe work environments, long hours, and poor compensation. Unions gave workers a voice and some political clout. That is as it *should* be in a democracy.

So why do I bring up unions? Because the teachers unions in this country are one of the greatest impediments to real educational progress. I'm not talking about the teachers here. Those men and women are engaged in a noble profession with difficult working conditions and far too little pay. Unfortunately, their unions have evolved into special interest groups where the product is no longer the priority. What matters most to unions are teachers' benefits, and that approach loses sight of the mission: our kids.

Former Colorado representative Bob Beauprez conducted an interesting examination of American teachers unions vs. their European counterparts. Believe it or not, Beauprez writes:

> *"Teachers unions in France, England, and Japan are much more powerful than their American counterparts. Leaders of teachers unions in France truthfully boast that they can put a million people in the streets of Paris to back their salary and benefit demands. In England, the National Union of Teachers vastly exceeds the legendary power of the British mine workers. Yet in none of these countries are the teachers unions the dangerous obstacle to student progress and quality teaching that they are in America."*

Why? European teachers unions had their origins in the ancient guilds or craft associations. These associations, Beauprez writes:

> *"… understood the fundamental link between good work and good pay."* They also knew that to produce good work you needed good *workers who were well trained. As a result, becoming a teacher in Europe involves a demanding admissions process with focused university training, constant testing, and an apprenticeship prior to joining the profession.*

That's not to say some of this doesn't exist in the United States. My good friend Catherine Dunn is the president emerita at Clarke

College in Dubuque, Iowa. Clarke has a wonderful series of apprenticeship programs called the Professional Development Schools, where students practice teaching in a supervised setting as they learn about elementary, secondary, and special education. But there's not enough of this, and, by and large, teachers unions are resistant to innovation.

The reason, Beauprez said, is that the American teachers unions used organizations like the United Auto Workers or the Teamsters as their union models—and that's one of the reasons I believe they are so ineffective. Think about it. By using these models, they missed an important nuance. The UAW and the Teamsters were representing factory workers. Understandably, the union's role was to protect the employees working in what can be harsh and hazardous work conditions. Product quality was not their concern, and it still isn't. That's the concern of management. But can a teachers union not be concerned about product quality and still produce a good product? I don't think so ... well, apparently not! The first thing the teachers unions need to understand is that just doing the easy job—you know, lobbying for better benefits, for instance—isn't enough. In my estimation it's about 10 percent of the job. They are the leadership, and as leaders they are getting failing grades.

But why should they care? The American teachers unions know they are at an advantage. While allowing product quality to decline and lowering the standards year after year would doom any business, it seems like the education system is still maintaining their "market share." There are still plenty of children with great minds and great capacity walking through the doors every day. No decline in the business of education, no worries there. Of course, that's because there is no competition for public education. Sure, there are private schools, charter schools, and more and more parents choosing to home school their children—but the number of children who are opting out of the public school system amount to less than a blip on the radar screen.

Not only does poor product quality still yield plenty of students, there are no financial repercussions either! What business has that luxury? Until the Bush administration created No Child Left Behind (NCLB), school districts knew they were going to be funded, no matter how poorly they performed. Even under NCLB, poorly performing school districts are only in danger of losing a portion of their federal funding, not the whole thing. And they all still receive state and local subsidies. I mean, this is the most ridiculous system ever. You can come to work, do your job poorly, produce a bad product consistently, lower your standards consistently, and still get paid. Given these realities, it's easy to see why our teachers unions are resistant to higher standards and incentive-based pay. They will actually be held accountable to performance, and who would want that? That's work!

Clearly, we need to get the teachers unions on board. But they are not going to come quietly. Kicking and screaming might be involved, and we will need to apply some heavy pressure:

Pressure from Parents—You may think this doesn't apply to you because, after all, your child gets all A's. But all A's compared to who? The child in the next chair, or the child in China who is getting all As? Here's a wake-up call. We live in a global economy today. Imagine what competition will be like when little Justin or little Hayley are all grown up. They will be competing with the person in China, Estonia, Japan, Canada, and a multitude of other countries.

Pressure from Politicians—I know, you have a lot on your plate, particularly judging from this book. But you have a lot of people working in Washington. Why not use this book as a guide and focus, focus, focus on the top issues and the simple solutions? The unions aren't going to change without some type of government action.

Pressure from the Media—Where's the Lou Dobbs of education? He made immigration his own personal platform, for better or worse, and there are plenty of mouthpieces out there for one political party or the other. Where's the mouthpiece for education? It's time this issue gets some media attention and a champion who is willing to take on the 300-pound gorilla.

Pressure from Teachers—In many cases, you're getting most of the blame, undeservedly. Don't you want to provide the best possible education and see your students achieve beyond where even they think they can go? Don't you have even the slightest amount of competitive spirit to say, "I want American kids to be the best educated kids in the world"? If you can't answer yes to all these questions, you should find another profession. But I believe most of you can say yes. Unite and push your union *toward* the future, not back. Work with management to creatively solve the problems you face. Education reform is top down, but the most change will happen bottom up. It all starts with you.

The Best and the Brightest Cost Money

American teachers have been underpaid for as long as I can remember. As I stated earlier, there is no profession more vital to the future of our nation than teaching, yet we pay experienced teachers like we would pay an entry-level employee in an investment bank. The reason for this is simple. Public education is publicly funded. There is no market mechanism with which to create more revenue, aside from maybe adding a few students to your enrollment figures. There is only so much money to go around, so teacher compensation can't increase dramatically … unless you get creative.

I believe the way to increase teachers' salaries is by putting less money into school buildings and facilities, and more into incentive-based compensation. I don't think you need to spend more for education; I think you need to spend the existing money wisely. Take a look at our schools today. While many have large classes of thirty or more students because we can't afford to pay for more teachers, many of those same schools have classrooms that sit empty for most of the day—the product of shifting populations in neighborhoods and poor, wasteful management on the part of school districts.

When a neighborhood no longer has students to fill all of its classrooms, that district should consolidate its schools by busing kids in from other neighborhoods, or, in the case of extreme student population decreases, close schools altogether. This is a political hot potato, because parents don't want to see their neighborhood school closed. They like the convenience of having their kids close to home. They like knowing their kids' teachers and coaches. They don't want to start all over again. But if we can make parents see the bigger picture—that efficient management leads to better teaching and better education—I think they'll come around. If we manage our schools more efficiently, we can pay teachers better salaries, thereby attracting better candidates while encouraging the existing ones to strive for greater results.

This line of thinking is already gaining steam with our newest secretary of education, Arne Duncan, and I hope he succeeds with his plan. Efficient management benefits any business structure, even if it's public education. The other half of Duncan's plan is incentive-based pay, a notion that whips teachers unions into a frenzy. I understand the union's trepidation. An incentive-based structure that isn't properly implemented could be disastrous. We can't have teachers tailoring their courses to specific, standardized tests unless those tests are broad enough and comprehensive enough to be certain our kids are learning everything they should learn.

But if incentive-based pay is implemented correctly, there is no reason to avoid it. Performance, and nothing else, should drive pay. I know a lot of teachers believe tenure is an insurance policy for older teachers who make good money. At the college level, tenure is vital to promote scholarly inquiries and lines of research that professors might otherwise avoid for fear of controversy that could get them fired. With K-12 tenure, older teachers argue it prevents them from being weeded out easily by a district official playing office politics, or a district looking to cut costs. But in a survey of teachers conducted recently by The Heartland Institute:

"58 percent of the teachers admitted that being awarded tenure does not necessarily mean such teachers have worked hard and proved

themselves to be very good at what they do. One union official even admitted to defending tenured teachers 'who shouldn't even be pumping gas.'"

Now I don't doubt that some district officials might play favorites and get rid of some of their best teachers for less than noble reasons. But that happens in every line of business, and those teachers still have legal recourse. Just as important—if we are holding districts to higher educational standards—it's not in the best interest of a district official to let his most talented teachers go. If he does, he won't be meeting those standards.

Another problem with tenure is that teachers who gain it tend to dictate where they will teach. If your district is efficient and has only awarded tenure to its best teachers, that means the talent will be unevenly distributed, with the best and most experienced teachers only working in optimal settings. Maybe that's not all bad, since people should have a say in where they work—but it certainly doesn't achieve the greater goal of public education.

Michelle Rhee, chancellor of the District of Columbia Public School system, recently proposed an incentive-based plan to that area's teachers union. In exchange for giving up tenure and surviving a one-year trial period, teachers could make up to $130,000 in merit pay based on their effectiveness. Alternately, they could keep tenure and accept a smaller raise, while all new teachers would be placed on the tenure-free track. The plan has the support of the Obama administration and Secretary of Education Arne Duncan, who announced a $297-million Teacher Incentive Fund this summer to reward teachers and principals nationwide for increases in student achievement. If Rhee's plan succeeds, it could revolutionize public education and take us a step in the right direction.

Higher Standards, National Standards

When President George W. Bush signed No Child Left Behind into law, the goals were admirable. NCLB identified a fundamental problem in the way schools districts reported test scores and measured achievement. The scores were too broad in scope. While breakdowns of individual schools were available, snapshots of the various demographics within those schools were not. As a result, if a district had four good schools and two poor schools, the overall picture would look pretty good, and everyone slapped each other on the back for a job well done.

NCLB requires districts to separate the test scores of their most at-risk populations—lower income families, disadvantaged minorities, and special needs students—to insure no children are being lost in the overall picture. Better yet, if districts are unable to meet standards set forth by NCLB—for at-risk students and all other students—they lose a portion of their federal funding. That's called an incentive, and it hadn't existed prior to NCLB.

There are a few problems with NCLB, however. First, in order to bring those at-risk students up to NCLB's standards, districts need more money. Education is often viewed as a low priority in at-risk populations. These communities lack the resources to correct that problem. Put simply, when parents and peers don't care about education, why should a child care? In order to change that culture, districts need more and better teachers, they need tutors, and they need community outreach programs to instill a climate of educational importance in at-risk communities. NCLB doesn't provide that funding. In fact, most states say federal funding has been less than what was promised—and far less than what is needed.

Here we go again. If the federal government is going to issue a mandate, then it had better fund it. Education is another victim of the ever-popular unfunded mandates. Again, I think more efficient spending will help in this regard. School districts are wasteful, and they need to be held more accountable by the state auditor-general offices and the state legislatures. The latter spends too much time pandering to its constituents and not enough time enacting meaningful change. But the federal government also has to carry its weight, instead of leaving cash-strapped states to foot the bill.

The other significant problem with NCLB is that there are no national standards for education. Secretary Duncan is pressuring states to change this, but the result of his efforts is not yet determined. Currently, NCLB wants students to achieve certain benchmarks, but it is up to the individual states to determine those benchmarks. As long as America has existed, this has been each state's right, and it's one that won't be forfeited lightly. To an extent, this is understandable. Some states, like Arizona, have far greater challenges ahead of them to meet national standards. With large Hispanic and Native American populations come vast cultural differences. Arizona faces a much tougher road to national standards than a Midwestern state like Iowa.

There are practical solutions, however. For one, we can create an acceptable range of scores within those standards, instead of one benchmark. We should also consider mitigating circumstances when punishing states that don't achieve these minimum standards. But those circumstances should be scrutinized with a fine-toothed comb to make sure we're not letting too much slide. National standards are important for many reasons. They hold school districts accountable for all students. They provide a yardstick by which we can measure ourselves against the world, and they put everyone on equal footing when they hit college or the workplace. Colleges and businesses will benefit because they won't have to waste time and money teaching remedial skills that should have been learned in the K-12 years.

Technology, Online Training, and Innovation

Our school districts spend too few dollars on technology-based education, and far too much on buildings. As I stated earlier when discussing incentive-based teacher salaries, this needs to change. We can't afford empty classrooms and palatial high schools without first providing our students an exceptional education. Technology-based innovations represent an area where America still leads the world. So why aren't we doing everything in our power to buy more computers; better, state-of-the-art software; and any other technological innovation that might help us maintain our edge?

This idea applies both to our curriculum and our teaching methods. Lots of people believe that if class sizes grow, the effectiveness of instruction will drop. Yet many of the world's nations have larger classes and still achieve higher test scores than we do in America. One area that could help in this regard is online education. The University of Phoenix, for example, provides an excellent model for how this can be applied to undergraduate and graduate studies. Other universities, that got their act together, have followed their lead and implemented similar online degree programs.

I believe this same idea can be applied to the K-12 levels. Not only would it be a more cost-effective approach (we wouldn't need as much classroom space), it would allow for flexibility in the scheduling of both teachers and the students, and it would allow for more in-depth instruction, because each student's queries could be answered by the teacher in written form, or via video conferencing. Online instruction might also promote better parental involvement, since the parents would be on hand when the child signs on from home, making them a part of the daily educational process. There's a lot of home schooling going on out there already, and those parents have to follow some sort of curriculum. Why not expand the online possibilities?

Speaking of innovative teaching methods, who was it that said the average school day has to be from 8 a.m. until 2 or 3 p.m.? Why can't we have longer school days? Most nations have longer school days, and most nations have better test scores than us. Is there a correlation? Probably. Parents are always saying how much energy their kids have—are we afraid we're going to tire kids out by adding an extra hour to school? It's a logical leap to assume more instruction equals better learning. Practice makes perfect, right? And why can't our kids go to school in the summer? The Chandler, Arizona, school district has year-round classes with periodic two- to three-week breaks to allow the kids to recharge their batteries. Why should teachers get summers off? I don't get *my* summers off. Neither does most of the working world.

And who says college has to be four years? Why can't it be three? Where do we come up with all these assumptions, and why don't enough people challenge them? We need innovative thinking to revamp and revitalize our educational system. We need the entrepreneurial spirit infused into our schools. Nothing should be above reexamination, and nothing should be immune to the chopping block if it's not helping better educate our kids. I get excited just thinking about it.

Continuing Education

Speaking of false assumptions, why do so many of us assume that once our high school, college, or graduate careers end, school is out? Many businesses have already discovered the importance of continuing education to train their employees. It's a fast-paced world out there, and the rate of technological advancement is increasing exponentially. A journalist friend of mine told me there is research to indicate that by the time journalism students reach the fourth year of their college education, the information they learned in their first year will be largely obsolete.

We must continually train our workforce to update them with the latest technological advancements, managerial strategies, and innovative ideas. We should never stop learning or we will lose our edge in the world market.

Summary

When I look back on some of the best teachers I had—guys like Art Volk, my accounting instructor at the University of South Dakota—there are several common threads. Their lessons were simple and clear, they always had time to help, and they were always aware of the latest ideas in their fields.

Teachers are the backbone of our educational system. Without them, nothing else is possible. So let's find ways to compensate them fairly, train them properly, and support them fully with curricula, technology, and tests that make sense. If we do this, we'll achieve two very important outcomes: the education of our children and a bright future for our nation.

CHAPTER 9

SAVING THE ECONOMY

Our issue is jobs,
Not handouts or grants.
Let us earn our way;
We are ready to build.

Any way you slice it, 2009 was a tough year for the economy. Some could argue that it wasn't that bad … after all, the stock market was up. But did you know that for the first time in recorded history, even with the 2009 boost, the S&P index ended the decade below where it started? And not just a little bit below, a lot below—more than 25 percent below. Even the decade of the Great Depression ended on a better note than that.

Although the stock market was up and did everything it could to try to recover the year and the decade, just about everything else went the wrong way. The biggest issue from the citizen's viewpoint was— and still is—the job market. At the writing of this book, U.S. unemployment is approximately 10 percent. And there is no blue-sky projection that that number will be declining significantly any time soon. In addition, the government spending levels and the rapidly growing federal deficit are making an already shell-shocked public even more nervous. It seems the only people not bothered by the numbers are the people inside the "Beltway." Do they know something we don't know?

The Obama administration and Congress see the biggest problems they face as being Cap and Trade and the health care bill. Okay, those are important—but if we don't face and fix the tough issues with the economy, those two big problems will only get bigger. We seem to have a slight disconnect (slight, my foot) between the general public (a.k.a. voters), and the people who are supposed to represent us (a.k.a. our elected officials). Do we have to shout from the steps of the Capitol, "Hey, stop spending money you don't have. Stop bailing out big companies. Start creating jobs outside of government, and kick this economy into gear!"? If they happen to be listening, they may actually ask us for a few ideas. Well, good thing if they do—I have a few for them, and for you. Just in case you find yourself on the Capitol steps, here goes.

Three Possible Directions for The Economy

The U.S. economy is complex, but resuscitating it doesn't have to be. You'll find my solutions are quite simple and have the power to build our economy back up in 2010 and 2011.

Economists, business analysts, and industry experts will tell you that there are a lot of ways our economy can go. Some of the predictions they report are hopeful. Others are dire, and several are somewhere in between. But it seems that most of the dialog is about three specific scenarios, none of which are certainties. The three are as follows:

1. Moderate growth and low or moderate inflation. A hopeful picture, this is the best possible scenario.

2. Hyper-inflation, which means prices rise as the value of our currency declines because the Federal Reserve floods too much currency into the world market.

3. Depression is the third scenario, and that means that our economy comes to a screeching halt, with prices falling because no one can buy. Sounds kind of familiar, doesn't it? We came very close in 2008. And we're not out of the woods yet.

I am not making any predictions, but I do know this: "Washington, we have a problem." And we are all concerned that no one in our capitol knows what to do about it. One thing we *do* know is that the direction our government is headed isn't cutting it. We can't spend our way out of this. We can't print money and expect to climb out of the hole we're in. You also can't create more government jobs and expect that to stimulate the economy. While you guys and gals get it figured out, here are some suggestions that will give the first scenario—the tolerable one—the best chance of happening.

Reduce the Deficit

This has to be job one, don't you agree? Most Americans do, and they also agree that it's going to take discipline and a commitment by our government to the following "must-do" list:

1. Quit spending
2. Approve the military budget
3. Cut everything else to the bone
4. %^(#@%#$! quit spending (Can this be any clearer?)
5. Reduce all administration and congressional salaries by 20 percent

Please, we need you leaders in Washington to show some leadership. Nearly everyone in this country is taking a hit. There have been layoffs, big losses in pensions and investments, company failures, home foreclosures ... people are hurting. But what about government employees, particularly the ones in Washington? Have there been layoffs similar to those in the private sector? Has the government, like business, reduced its spending on new programs or looked for ways to cut expenses? Have they looked for ways to work smarter with less overhead and produce the same results? No, government has not.

You may be surprised to learn that government has been increasing its workforce—not reducing it. According to the Bureau of Labor Statistics, the private sector lost approximately 3.65 million jobs in 2008, while the government increased jobs by almost 150,000 in the same period. That trend appears to have continued well into 2010. Since these statistics were reported by CNN in early 2009, more government jobs have been added to carry out programs designed to stimulate the economy. Hello? You don't stimulate a private-sector economy by creating government jobs. Fine, create programs if you want, but hire public-sector companies to put them into action. That's what will stimulate the economy; beefing up the government only stimulates the government.

Our leaders in Washington have complained about the fat-cat bankers, as well as the businesspeople who use executive jets and appear to spend money recklessly. But what are we getting from those who are pointing fingers? As any businessperson will tell you, throwing money and people at a problem will not solve the problem, it will only make it worse. And in my eyes, that's what we have going on here in Washington. Instead of looking at our problems and solving them with brainpower, we've got the Federal Reserve printing presses going into overtime and every government official hiring their friends. That's not how you run a business; it shouldn't be how our elected leaders run this country. This madness has to stop.

Support and Assist Entrepreneurial and Small Business Development

This is called the President John Kennedy, President Ronald Reagan, and Jim Houtz (your author) plan. I have acknowledged two former presidents whom I greatly admire and each implemented some or all of the following items. My contribution is putting them together, and then asking why we have not already done something similar. Their plans worked and they can work again.

If I didn't make it clear earlier in this book, allow me to restate: The most powerful force we have in this country is the force of our entrepreneurs and small business owners. They and they alone have the ability to pull our economy up by its bootstraps and make it strong again. They, not government workers, are who should and must be empowered to innovate, grow, and develop new solutions to our problems.

When small business grows our economy grows, people get jobs, and new industries spring up that have the potential to change our world for the better. We could use a dose of that, don't you think, rather than a modern-day WPA (Work Progress Administration) from the 1940s? That's what we're getting now, at the expense of our future. Believe me, the great entrepreneurs of this country, who have yet to emerge, aren't going to work for the government. They are going to work for themselves and it's up to us to encourage them, and fast. Here's how—and this may look a little familiar, but it is worth repeating:

1. Significantly lower taxes on the first $200,000 of annual income for small business with less than 500 employees.

2. Establish a 10-percent business investment tax credit on all leased or purchased equipment for all business entities.

3. Lower taxes on first $1 million of annual income for all business entities that manufacture or assemble products in the United States.

4. Dramatically expand the SBA (Small Business Administration) loan availability.

5. Develop employee-hiring bonus that gives the employer an amount equal to 20 percent of first-year compensation for each new employee the company hires.

I revealed this plan in the chapter called Saving Entrepreneurship. But it is imperative. If the Obama administration knew about the success of both Kennedy and Reagan and how they dug us out of recessions, it surely would have implemented these measures by now. They worked! But then again, it's not hard to find people who have a perfectly good wheel and still feel the need to invent a new one. Maybe that's the case with our current leadership in Washington, but it appears the one they have invented isn't rolling very well.

Change the Fiscal Policy: Taxes vs. Spending

I've been in business for a long time, and I've never yet seen a company spend its way out of trouble. Maybe I'm just myopic, but I can't see how this country is going to spend its way out of our massive deficit. It's impossible. In all my years, I've also never seen a company succeed by treating its customers poorly. Furthermore, I've never seen a company rebound by raising the cost of goods and services to the point where the customer suffers. Well, that is exactly what is proposed by this administration. If you think of voters as customers (which they are) and you think of taxes as the cost of goods and services (which they are), then you can easily make this connection: Our government is attempting to pull our economy out of the woods by creating more hardship for its customers—in other words, for us!

I'll repeat my position again. Our leaders need to stop spending. And let me add to that: They need to get the idea of raising taxes out of their heads. In case you're tired of hearing this from me, let me share with you a few lines from some Harvard-ites who have done their homework. The following is an abstract from October 1, 2009, and last revised November 9, 2009, written by Alberto F. Alesina and Silvia Ardagna of the Harvard Institute of Economic Research. If you'd like to read the full report, it is Discussion Paper No. 2180. Here's what Mr. Alesina and Ms. Ardagna had to say:

"We examined the evidence on episodes of large stances in fiscal policy, both in cases of fiscal stimuli and in that of fiscal adjustments in OECD (Organization for Economic Cooperation and Development) countries from 1970 to 2007. Fiscal stimuli based upon tax cuts are more likely to increase growth than those based upon spending increases. As for fiscal adjustments, those based upon spending cuts and no tax increases are more likely to reduce deficits and debt over GDP ratios than those based upon tax increases. In addition, adjustments on the spending side rather than on the tax side are less likely to create recessions. We confirm these results with simple regression analysis."

The full report is available at the Social Science Research Network (www.SSRN.com), but I think you get the point. We can only pray that Congress gets it, too: that "fiscal stimuli based upon tax cuts are more likely to increase growth than those based upon spending increases."

Looks like Presidents Kennedy and Reagan knew what they were doing after all.

The report didn't cover how stimuli based upon tax cuts would compare with spending increases co-mingled with earmarks commonly known as pork. That probably throws the numbers and the trends even further in the wrong direction. This is what I am saying. We need some leadership in Washington, and we need it now. The problem is that what we predominantly have in Washington are puppets. There probably isn't a good time to talk about this, but if not now, when? What do you think happens if a senator secures an earmark of $100 million as a result of some vote he or she makes? Does that senator receive "compensation" for that in the form of a few million in campaign funds, or do they just receive bundles of hundred-dollar bills that they keep in the freezer? Hey, you have to keep it somewhere.

I'm being facetious, but we all know that a good earmark won doesn't go unrewarded. But in an era where the house of cards we call our economy is approaching the moment where one more joker played will topple the whole thing, you'd think our leaders in Congress would be true servants to the people who elected them and work to bolster and rebuild that card house, making it stronger and more equipped to handle hardship. Instead, they are looking to play their own cards and win the hand. I shake my head and wonder how things got this messed up. I also wonder who the jokers are—us for letting it happen, or them for having the nerve to keep up this game. In any case, we're not laughing.

Stop Unfunded Mandates

Our Congress just loves to do things for the people; they are public servants, after all. Congress especially loves doing things for people when they can figure out a way for the state governments to pay the tab. It's a fantastic concept for them: They get something valuable for us, they take the credit, and then we pay for it. If this concept is new to you, then consider Medicaid. The federal government only picks up half of the $200-billion tab to fund this program annually. This Unfunded Mandate Reform Act of 1995, as it was called, was put in place "to curb the practice of imposing unfunded Federal mandates on States and local Governments." That is the actual language in the bill. But since then our Congress has worked diligently and has found a way to circumvent the law in more than one instance.

If you have followed the health care debate, then you may be aware of the "Nebraska Compromise." In December, MSNBC and other news organizations reported of a deal that was struck with Democratic senator Ben Nelson that permanently exempts his state of Nebraska from paying the Medicaid costs that all other states must pay. This was in exchange for his crucial sixtieth vote, which was needed to pass the massive health care bill. It was a pretty good deal for Nelson, but not so good for all of us who live in other states who now have to foot Nebraska's Medicaid along with our own.

You know, once this was out of the bag, it would create a frenzy. It did. Now, instead of solving our health care problems or bolstering our economy, we're keeping attorneys general busy, since several states have deemed the whole deal unconstitutional. And we wonder why so little gets accomplished. I have heard several senators say their vote is not for sale. I guess Senator Nelson's is. And thanks to this wonderful display of integrity, we stall our future yet again and steer the dialogue away from the real issues to one of scandal.

Thank goodness someone took the high road and made sure only Nelson, and not Nebraska, got a black eye in the whole mess. Dave Heineman, governor of the state, went on television and said in essence that Nebraska doesn't want a special deal, they want a good deal, one that's good for all states, and this isn't it! In January of 2010, *The Huffington Post* reported that Senator Nelson asked congressional leaders to "eliminate the controversial Medicaid deal from the health care bill."

I don't live in Nebraska, but Governor Heineman has earned my respect and admiration. He reminds me of the many good friends I have from Nebraska. But the Nebraska Compromise was just one of many special provisions in the health care bill. The Medicaid unfunded mandate has governors up in arms. Can't Congress see this kind of dealing gets us nowhere? No matter how you cut it, this needs to stop.

Solve CO_2 and Global Warming Without Busting the Economy

You might wonder how the issues of carbon dioxide (CO_2) and global warming ended up in the economy chapter. Well, these issues are here because the solutions that we pose to deal with them have the power to bring this country down or build it up. And contrary to what our politicians and former politicians (specifically Al Gore) tell us about the debate on global warming being over, that its existence is a given, I think it has just started. It appears there are a few facts which have not yet been resolved. For example:

1. Is the planet actually warming?
2. Is the warming actually caused by CO_2?
3. Is the data being used to measure the planet's temperature change reliable?
4. Will the solutions justify the cost?

I will not attempt to answer these questions here. That's a book all by itself. Actually volumes. But I do want you to know that I am very much in favor of improving our environment. I would like to have cleaner air and better water, just like most everyone would. But I don't like feeling duped, and I am concerned that the current direction and status is one of manipulation. How does a program that is supposed to help the environment come out of Washington as nothing more than a Trojan Horse designed to garner more tax revenue and seize control of the energy industry? It's called Cap and Trade. I'm all for solving the environmental problems and getting at their roots, but I don't like tax increases and loss of free enterprise being cloaked in the garments of environmental preservation. That's manipulative.

Now, back to the questions. The reality is, the answers don't matter within a conversation about saving the economy. What *does* matter is making sure that every dollar we spend, whether it be on the environment or education or everything in between, is spent wisely— not based on fear tactics, not based on bribes, and not based on an unproven sense of critical urgency.

Right now, based on a theory that many experts don't support, we are talking about spending trillions of dollars to implement a Cap and Trade program to limit carbon dioxide emissions. Based on how well our government has implemented the Troubled Asset Relief Program (TARP) and the various stimulus packages, I think we need a better plan that solves the right problem, which, as I stated earlier in this book, is our reliance on fossil fuels. We have to stop implementing bad programs badly. They hurt our economy.

A Crisis of Leadership

It's becoming all too obvious what *candidate* Barack Obama meant by "redistribution of wealth" now that he is *President* Barack Obama. It means they take more of our money, load us and our family members up with a bigger national debt, and, whenever possible, give our jobs to someone else. It seems the goal is to make everyone the same, and by the same, I mean poor. Do you feel you are getting what you voted for?

The *Investor's Business Daily* really put it on the line in their January 6, 2010, issue when they printed in their "Perspective" section an editorial appraising President Obama's first year in office. It was written by Ernest S. Christian, an attorney and former deputy assistant secretary of the treasury in the Ford administration; and Gary A. Robbins, an economist who served at the Treasury Department in the Reagan administration. Here are a few excerpts from the editorial:

"COMPARISONS OF OBAMA TO CARTER ARE INAPT AND UNFAIR (TO CARTER)

"Because of President Obama's outrageous profligacy with the public purse, strong policy tilt to the left and weak performance on the world stage, some commentators foresee a failed presidency that does profound and permanent harm to the nation.

"When he ran for president, Obama concealed his left-wing ideology, but true to its principles, eschewed the normally obligatory campaign obeisances to middle-class values and America's exceptional place in the firmament of nations. Instead, he talked about 'transforming' America and gulled about 60 million voters into thinking that change meant restoration, not destruction.

"Obama either doesn't understand, or doesn't like, free-market capitalism. He continues to prescribe high-risk government elixirs that, when administrated in greater quantities, will permanently damage the economy.

"Obama does, however, understand how to loot the American middle class with his on-rushing combination of monetary, tax and spending policies designed to rob them of $5 trillion to $10 trillion over a decade.

"The ObamaCare monstrosity, stuffed with pork and deception, claiming to do what it does not and pretending to do good while inflicting harm, is a national disgrace, an insult to the intelligence of every American and a fitting monument to President Obama's first year in office.

"Jimmy Carter was not the greatest, but he wasn't the worst president America has had. Barrack Obama is so far winning the race to the bottom."

Thank you, *Investor's Business Daily*. I do not like to hit someone when they are down, but President Obama is sinking fast. Right now, his popularity is down, his effectiveness is down, and the general populace has figured out that both his campaign persona and his proposed campaign direction are dramatically different than his first year in office. If he had campaigned for the program he has been implementing during his first year, I believe he would never have been even nominated, let alone elected.

The president has managed to pass some significant legislation, and it doesn't take a PhD to figure out that how it was accomplished. Do you think it has anything to do with money? Or more specifically earmarks? Let's call them what they are: payoffs or just outright bribes. At some point you have to label things correctly, and outside the "Beltway" we call them bribes.

It Will Not Be Easy From Here!

Considering the current dissatisfaction with our president and Congress, you might think that the next election in 2010 will be easy. My recommendation is to vote out all the big spenders. It's the answer, but I didn't say it was an easy answer. We all need to prepare for a very long, tough fight for all the congressional seats up for election in 2010. We can expect that more money than we can possibly imagine from the Stimulus Plan, earmarks, and existing campaign funds will flow into the campaigns, especially after the Supreme Court overthrew past legislation related to campaign finance in early 2010. In addition, we will see massive fraud in voter registration and significant disruptions in the voting polls. Both Democrats and Republicans will be affected by any election that is not run in an honest, well-managed election process.

This will be a knock-down, drag-out fight—as will every other election until we get these fundamental issues fixed. Get involved, speak the truth, fight with words and concepts for your ideals, and make sure we are not taken over by any person, group, party, or club who is not acting in the best interests of America.

This is a great country, and no one loves America more than I do. My plan is to help this country become greater. I have no interest in watching its demise. I want to see all young children have all the opportunities and chances for success that my colleagues and I have had. The first chance we will have for getting the country redirected to match up with the dreams of John F. Kennedy, Ronald Reagan, and Jim Houtz will be in the elections of 2010. America and the world will be dependent on your efforts. We are counting on you in the next elections and beyond.

Play hard, play fair, and if it's not working, play harder. Let's go, America! The world is watching. This is not a game; it is a fight for our freedom and for our very existence.

We will succeed; we will overcome!

WHAT SHOULD
WE DO NOW?

★★★★★★★★★★★★★★★★★★★★★★★

★★★★★★★★★★★★★★★★★★★★★★★★

CHAPTER 10

THE PATH FORWARD

The path forward
Is filled with potholes
Littered with pebbles
And incredible opportunities.

So where do we go from here? This book has covered a lot of issues and suggested a way to prioritize and solve them. Now it's time for the hard work it will take to fix what ails this country. This is how I see the path forward, along with the many obstacles that will get in the way of Saving America.

The 2010 Elections Outlook

The Republicans, Democrats, and Tea Parties will be actively campaigning for their beliefs and policies. Here's how they will side:

Democrats' message: "It's George Bush's fault."

Republicans' message: "They (the Democrats) are spending too much."

Tea Parties' message: Varied depending on the political party alignment, but mostly, "Can you people listen to us and get something done?"

The White House Outlook

It's been a little over a year since the Obama administration took office. They have surprised (read: dumbfounded) the American public by how far to the left they have governed. They passed a $1-trillion (yes, *trillion*) stimulus bill that was supposed to create jobs, and hasn't. It also included massive earmarks and significant political payoffs. They increased the deficit to approximately $1.8 trillion. And, in my estimation, broke most of their campaign promises. They've done no better than any administration before them; they have played the "Washington Way" by using bribes to pass legislation. I gave this practice its own name, because that's the only place where you can behave so heinously and not go to jail. That's enough disappointment, don't you think? I believe this will only continue for the remainder of President Obama's term.

2010 Election Democratic Party Outlook

Every midterm election almost always sees the majority party suffering losses in both the House and the Senate. The election in 2010 will be no exception, and Democrats are very concerned that the losses will be significant. In all probability, they will lose several seats in the Senate, and the two parties will actually have to talk and compromise to get any business done. That's actually the way it's supposed to be. The same goes for the House.

On December 30, 2009, Jonathan Martin published an article on the POLITICO website (www.politico.com) entitled "Anxious Dems Divide Over Path Forward." He quoted William Daley, commerce secretary in the Clinton administration, as follows:

> *"Either we plot a more moderate, centrist course or risk electoral disaster not just in the upcoming midterm but in many elections to come." Democrats ought to "acknowledge that the agenda of the party's most liberal supporters has not won the support of a majority of Americans—and, based on that recognition, they'll need to steer a more moderate course on the key issues of the day, from health care to the economy to the environment to Afghanistan."*

Those in the party who contend that such a move to a moderate position would demoralize their base, challenge Daley's position. I am sure they will figure it out. Good thing the Republicans don't have those kinds of direction problems. Oh yeah? Dream on!

2010 Election Republican Party Outlook

The Republicans are just as messed up as the Democrats. They seem very excited about their candidates' chances for 2010. I can't for the life of me see why. I fail to see anything legitimate they have done to earn a significant resurgence. I'm surprised by the fact that, at the time of this writing, they have not spelled out some type of plan that differentiates themselves from their opponents. That's what Newt Gingrich did several years ago and, after getting a majority elected, proceeded to implement all but one of his objectives.

Instead of offering leadership, the current Republican mantra for getting elected seems to be, "I am not a Democrat." Even though that might be good enough for those people who don't like to think much, it isn't good enough for me. I am not voting for anyone who cannot make a commitment to do the following:

1. Balance our budget and get rid of the deficit
2. Eliminate earmarks
3. Push for legislation to eliminate bribes, specifically buying votes
4. Develop an entrepreneurial and small business plan with simple incentives for achievement

In addition, the Republicans seem to be quick to point fingers at the Obama administration for overspending. But neither I nor the majority of Americans have forgotten the Republican's own lack of fiscal responsibility the last time they were in charge. Can they be trusted with the Treasury if given another chance? I'm not convinced.

2010 New Party, Tea Party Outlook

The Tea Parties are amazing and exciting. They have drawn crowds and gotten people actively involved in government again. It's quite inspirational. As I said in one of the earlier chapters, before you can solve a problem, you need to realize you have one. The Tea Party participants know we have a problem and are trying to do something about it.

Some people think the Tea Party could morph into a viable third party. At the right time, I think it would make sense. However, we have a more pressing issue right now, which is: What happens if the White House and Congress are allowed to continue their current path for an additional two years beyond the 2010 election? I think the country would be a disaster, and the great place we call America would be diminished beyond repair. Our financial system would be destroyed, our freedoms diminished, and our dreams obliterated. This last year has reminded me what a great country we have, and I want to keep it as it was prior to 2009.

I think the Tea Parties have been beneficial to our country, and I think a Tea Party majority would be fantastic. Here is a very simplistic plan of how to move towards a viable third party.

- **2010 Elections**

  Vote all the big spenders from both parties out. Develop a Tea Party objective list and ask senators and congressmen to commit to it. Most probably will not, but some will—and these could potentially be your leaders when the time is right.

- **2011 Post Election**

  Begin working for the 2012 election. Register the party in every state. Ask acceptable members of Congress to join. Recruit new candidates for each state.

- **Prepare for Election**

  Select presidential candidate or commit to support one major party candidate.

It's a simple plan. But here's the catch. If we do not accomplish our objective of voting the big spenders out, we will not have a chance to do any of the rest. Good luck.

The U.S. Dollar Outlook

The U.S. dollar is gradually losing its purchasing power. Every time the Fed prints more money, they devalue our currency. A possible next step would be to devalue our currency in one shot. We did this before—during the 1930s Depression, when we went temporarily off the gold standard. I hope rapid devaluation doesn't happen again, because it would create utter chaos.

Our best plan is too fix our deficit, making whatever cuts are necessary. Fix our economy by getting the small business people and entrepreneurs going again. They provide the most jobs and are the backbone of our nation.

Employment Outlook

We all need to be concerned about some of the forecasts predicting that our recovery will be one without significant job growth. I hope not! I would ask existing companies to consider the following to see if you can generate some additional jobs.

1. When hiring, consider splitting jobs where appropriate and hire two part-timers instead of one full-time person

2. Hire some additional salespeople on a straight commission

3. Consider any products, U.S. or foreign built, that you could build here in the U.S.

4. Consider a group healthcare plan that allows the employee to pay the first few dollars with company-provided funds (which will save the company money)

5. Re-negotiate all your contracts with vendors

6. Consider taking your products or services into new markets

7. Consider licensing your products to companies in other geographical markets

8. Bring in house the services you typically farm out

My second entrepreneurial book, *Grow the Entrepreneurial Dream*, is available online. Visit my website, www.jimhhoutz.com, to read chapters and excerpts, and share your thoughts. Your comments may make it into the printed and e-book editions due out in the fall of 2010. It will also be available on Amazon.com

Hot Issues in the 2010 Election

No election these days is without its hot issues. I can see them coming. Get set for some in these areas:

- **Ethics in Politics**

  This is not a case of creating better ethics. We are at ground zero; we will take any indication of ethics for the House and Senate. I mean, just look around. All the money spent buying votes on the health care bill alone should make my case.

- **Health Care**

  The health care bill may or may not pass by the time of the election. If passed, you can use our health care chapter to rescind or modify the bill. If it is not passed, the chapter would be a good foundation to create, develop, and pass a solid health care bill for all Americans—one without special deals, special programs, and/or preferential treatment.

- **Economy**

  The White House and Congress need to understand there are two ways to expand the economy. One is a right and productive way, and the other is a way that spends a massive amount of money for minimal results. To maximize your energy and impact, please read or re-read the chapters in this book on entrepreneurship and the economy.

Proceed With Caution

As we proceed on "The Path Forward," we need to proceed with caution—and make sure our direction (or path) is consistent with the Constitution. There are a considerable number of individuals in both parties who consider themselves progressives. They believe the Constitution does not go far enough and are gradually pushing us towards socialism. Approximately 85 members of Congress—both Republicans and Democrats—consider themselves progressives, and want government to become bigger and take on more responsibility. In addition, the White House has more than its fair share of progressives on its staff of czars.

In her August 31, 2009 "Watchdog Politics" column on Examiner.com, Martha Gore wrote,

> *"As Americans learn more about Obama's efforts to circumvent the Constitution and Bill of Rights, it has created a wake up call among the population. As more of his past is exposed, and the realization of exactly who is in his Shadow Government, and that the most precious word in the American vocabulary, 'freedom,' is at risk."*

Ronald Reagan said,

> *"Freedom is never more than one generation away from extinction. We didn't pass it to our children in the bloodstream. It must be fought for, protected, and handed on for them to do the same, or one day we will spend our sunset years telling our children and children's children what it was once like in the United States where men were free."*

I would like to think that Ronald Reagan would approve and endorse this book. Just as importantly, I hope you do—and I encourage you to join all those Americans who are engaged in the fight for freedom. The fight for saving America.

About the Author

Jim Houtz—entrepreneur, venture capitalist, author, Washington watcher and former CEO—believes that the problems our nation and the world face today can be solved not by government programs, but by entrepreneurs. From our reliance on foreign oil and our out-of-control health care costs to our challenged education system and our faltering economy, Houtz sees American ingenuity through entrepreneurship as the answer. Houtz believes entrepreneurs will be the ones who develop the products, the services, and the innovations that will save our world—unless, of course, big government gets in the way. Houtz's mission is to stop our government from stacking the deck in favor of special interests, and instead promote free-market competition. He sees his role as one of enlightening a new breed of entrepreneurs to the Washington shenanigans that can crush their businesses. He considers it his job to inspire these men and women to stand up for their futures.

A lifelong entrepreneur himself, Houtz was the founder of CyCare, the nation's number one group practice management software company that he sold to HBOC in 1996. Today he works with entrepreneurs and entrepreneurial companies to help them grow their businesses for their own gain and for the survival of our nation. Houtz accomplishes this through his interactive website, JimHHoutz.com, which covers news on entrepreneurship, business building, and government policy affecting business. This website is also where Houtz is in the process of releasing—chapter by chapter, at no charge—his new book *Grow the Entrepreneurial Dream: How to Take Your Business from Start-Up to World-Class*, which follows on the heals of his first and highly acclaimed book *Seize the American Dream: 10 Entrepreneurial Success Strategies*. *Saving America: Common Sense Solutions to Washington Nonsense* is Houtz's third book, which tackles the eight biggest issues we must solve and poses entrepreneurial solutions for each of them. It simplifies and prioritizes our challenges and provides common sense solutions that are actionable by people who know how to take action: entrepreneurs. Together, the website, the books, and Jim's outspoken yet thoughtful demeanor pack the power we need as a nation to move forward in our new century.

Works Cited

"1970s Energy Crisis." *Wikipedia*. Web. 8 Feb. 2010
<http://en.wikipedia.org/wiki/1970s_Energy_Crisis>.

"1979 Energy Crisis." *Wikipedia*. Web. 11 Feb. 2010
<http://en.wikipedia.org/wiki/1979_energy_crisis>.

"Advantages of Biofuels." *Want to Know It?* Web. 12 Feb. 2010
<http://wanttoknowit.com/advantages-of-biofuels/>.

Aikin, Blaine. "Congress abdicates its fiduciary duty." *Investment News*.
5 Oct. 2008. Web. 5 Feb. 2010 <http://www.investmentnews.com/apps/
pbcs.dll/article?AID=/20081005/REG/310069989&ht=congress%20abdi-
cates%20its%20fiduciary%20duty>.

Aleklett, Klejj. "Dick Cheney, Peak Oil and the Final Countdown."
www.peakoil.net. 12 May 2004. Web. 12 Feb. 2010
<http://www.peakoil.net/Publications/Cheney_PeakOil_FCD.pdf>.

All Academic Inc. Web. 11 Feb. 2010 <http://www.allacademic.com/>.

Anselmo, Joe. "USAF Launches Major Biofuel Initiative."
www.aviationweek.com. 30 Jan. 2009. Web. 8 Feb. 2010 <http://www.avia-
tionweek.com/aw/generic/story_generic.jsp?channel=aerospacedaily&id=n
ews/BIOF013009.xml&headline=USAF Launches Major Biofuel
Initiative>.

Arizona Office of the Auditor General Home Page. Web. 12 Feb. 2010
<http://www.auditorgen.state.az.us/>.

Arpaio, Sheriff Joe, and Len Sherman. *Joe's Law: America's Toughest Sheriff
Takes on Illegal Immigration, Drugs and Everything Else That Threatens
America*. New York: AMACOM, 2008. Amazon Kindle edition.

Asher, Michael. "Latest Research Erodes CO2's Role in Global Warming."
DailyTech.com. 24 Aug. 2007. Web. 8 Feb. 2010 <http://www.dailytech.com/
Latest+Research+Erodes+CO2s+Role+in+Global+Warming/article8588.htm>.

Bank, Justin. "Cost of Illegal Immigrants." *FactCheck.org*. 6 Apr. 2009.
Web. 11 Feb. 2010 <http://www.factcheck.org/2009/04/cost-of-illegal-
immigrants/>.

Bartlett, Donald L., and James B. Steele. "America's Border." *TIME Magazine*. Web. 11 Feb. 2010 <http://www.time.com/time/covers/1101040920/>.

"Ben E. Keith Beverages first distributor in U.S. to 'Go Green' with first hybrid beverage tractor." *Coopersmithagency.com*. 10 Feb. 2009. Web. 8 Feb. 2010 <http://coopersmithagency.com/2009/02/10/ben-e-keith-beverages-first-distributor-in-us-to-go-green-with-first-hybrid-beverage-tractor/>.

"Ben Nelson Asks Senate Leaders To Delete Nebraska Medicaid Deal From Final Health Care Bill." *Huffingtonpost.com*. 15 Jan. 2010. Web. 11 Feb. 2010 <http://www.huffingtonpost.com/2010/01/15/ben-nel-son-asks-senate-le_n_425304.html>.

Biofuelscenter.org. Web. 8 Feb. 2010 <http://www.biofuelscenter.org/index.cfm?page=content&scid1=38& CategoryID=14>.

"Biomass Energy Sources for Alternative Electricity Production." *Bionomicfuel.com*. Web. 8 Feb. 2010 <http://www.bionomicfuel.com/biomass-energy-sources-for-alternative-electricity-production/>.

"Biomass vs. Coal." *Mindfully.org*. Web. 8 Feb. 2010 <http://www.mindfully.org/Energy/Biomass-vs-Coal.htm>.

"Bipartisan Campaign Reform Act of 2002." *Federal Election Commission Home Page*. Web. 11 Feb. 2010 <http://www.fec.gov/pages/bcra/bcra_ update.shtml>.

Blumenthal, Les. "Aviation biofuel proves itself in tests, but is there enough?" *McClatchydc.com*. 28 May 2009. Web. 8 Feb. 2010 <http://www.mcclatchydc.com/251/story/69028.html>.

Book, Robert A., and David M. Cutler. "Issue Clash: Will health care reform be effective in reducing health care costs?" *PBS.org*. Web. 8 Feb. 2010 <http://www.pbs.org/now/shows/health-care-reform/ic-health-care-costs.html>.

Braden, Brian. "U.S. military strength keeps global economy intact—Army Community—Army Discussions—Army Times." *Army News, benefits, careers, entertainment, photos, promotions—Army Times HOME*. Web. 5 Feb. 2010 <http://www.armytimes.com/community/opinion/army_backtalk_strength_012609/>.

Brown, Harold. "Chinese Military Power." *Council on Foreign Relations.*
May 2003. Web. 5 Feb. 2010
<http://www.cfr.org/publication/5985/chinese_military_power.html>.

Bruno, Greg. "The Future of the U.S. Military." *Council on Foreign
Relations.* 7 Nov. 2007. Web. 5 Feb. 2010
<http://www.cfr.org/publication/14721/future_of_the_us_military.html>.

Buchanan, Patrick J. *State of Emergency: The Third World Invasion and Conquest
of America.* New York: St. Martin's Press, 2006. Amazon Kindle edition.

Burd, Steven. "How Safeway Is Cutting Health-Care Costs." *WSJ.com.*
12 June 2009. Web. 8 Feb. 2010
<http://online.wsj.com/article/SB124476804026308603.html>.

Byrnes, Ryan. "Private Sector Jobs Decline, Government Jobs Increase."
CNSNews.com. 9 Mar. 2009. Web. 11 Feb. 2010
<http://www.cnsnews.com/news/article/44662>.

Camarota, Steven A. "Immigrants at Mid-Decade." *Center for Immigration
Studies.* Dec. 2005. Web. 11 Feb. 2010
<http://www.cis.org/articles/2005/ back1405.html>.

Caminiti, Susan. "Preschool Around the Globe." *Fortune.* 21 Oct. 1991.
Web. 5 Feb. 2010 <http://money.cnn.com/magazines/fortune/fortune_
archive/1991/10/21/75605/index.htm>.

Campbell, Karen. "Killing the Entrepreneurial Spirit: Government Is Not
a Good Investor." *The Heritage Foundation - Conservative Policy Research and
Analysis.* 22 May 2009. Web. 5 Feb. 2010
<http://www.heritage.org/ research/economy/wm2455.cfm>.

"Celebrity Bankruptcies Throughout History." *Totalbankruptcy.com.* Web.
8 Feb. 2010
<http://www.totalbankruptcy.com/news/articles/celebrity/notables.aspx>.

Center for International Policy. Web. 12 Feb. 2010
<http://www.ciponline.org/>.

Chandler Unified School District. Web. 11 Feb. 2010
<http://ww2.chandler.k12.az.us/chandlerschools/site/default.asp>.

"China attacks US military report." *Council on Foreign Relations*. 28 May 2007. Web. 5 Feb. 2010 <http://www.cfr.org/publication/5985/ chinese_military_power.html>.

Christian, Ernest, and Gary Robbins. "Comparisons Of Obama To Carter Are Inapt And Unfair (To Carter)." *Investors.com*. 5 Jan. 2010. Web. 5 Feb. 2010 <http://www.investors.com/NewsAndAnalysis/Article.aspx? id=517116>.

Clark, Rebecca L., and Scott A. Anderson. "Illegal Aliens in Federal, State, and Local Criminal Justice Systems: Summary." *Urban.org*. 30 June 2000. Web. 11 Feb. 2010 <http://www.urban.org/publications/410366.html>.

COBRAInsurance.com. Web. 8 Feb. 2010 <http://cobrainsurance.com>.

ConsumerDrivenHealthCare.us: Guide to Options in Consumer Driven Health Care. Web. 5 Feb. 2010 <http://www.consumerdrivenhealthcare.us/>.

Cornell, Clayton B. "Biodiesel Mythbuster 2.0." *Gas2.org*. 10 Apr. 2008. Web. 8 Feb. 2010 <http://gas2.org/2008/04/10/biodiesel-mythbuster-20-twenty-two-biodiesel-myths-dispelled/>.

"Crossing the Border to Purchase Health Insurance | MedHealth News & Updates." *Medhealthinsurance.com*. 20 Oct. 2008. Web. 8 Feb. 2010 <http://www.medhealthinsurance.com/blog/purchasing-insurance-another-state/>.

"Cuban Missile Crisis: Summary." *Oracle ThinkQuest Library*. 1997. Web. 11 Feb. 2010 <http://library.thinkquest.org/11046/days/index.html>.

"Cuban Missile Crisis." *Wikipedia*. Web. 11 Feb. 2010 <http://en.wikipedia .org/ wiki/Cuban_Missile_Crisis>.

Draoua, Mehdi. "The Effect of Illegal Immigration on the US Healthcare System." *Hopkins Undergraduate Research Journal* 7 (2007). Print.

"Duct Tape Alert." *Wikipedia*. Web. 11 Feb. 2010 <http://en.wikipedia.org/ wiki/Duct_tape_alert>.

"Eat Right." *EverydayChoices.org*. Web. 5 Feb. 2010 <http://everydaychoices.org/eat.html>.

Education Week. Web. 11 Feb. 2010 <http://www.edweek.org/ew/index.html>.

"Fossil Fuel Phase Out." *Wikipedia*. Web. 8 Feb. 2010 <http://en.wikipedia. org/wiki/Fossil_fuel_phase_out>.

Foucher, Sam. "October 2006: Production Forecasts and EIA Oil Production Numbers." *TheOilDrum.com*. 16 Oct. 2006. Web. 8 Feb. 2010 <http://www.theoildrum.com/story/2006/10/3/104458/751>.

Frank, Thomas. "Illegal immigrant population declines." *www.usatoday.com*. 24 Feb. 2009. Web. 11 Feb. 2010 <http://www.usatoday.com/news/nation/2009-02-23-immigration_N.htm>.

Gallup.Com. 19 Dec. 2009. Web. 12 Feb. 2010 <http://www.gallup.com/home.aspx>.

"Glossary." *EcoagriculturePartners.com*. Web. 8 Feb. 2010 <http://www.ecoagriculture.org/page.php?id=65&name=Glossary>.

GoArmy.com. Web. 5 Feb. 2010 <http://www.goarmy.com/>.

"Great Depression." *Wikipedia*. Web. 11 Feb. 2010 <http://en.wikipedia.org/ wiki/Great_Depression#Gold_standard>.

"Great Plains—The Camelina Company Makes Camelina Biodiesel a Reality." *Businesswire.com*. 3 Sept. 2008. Web. 8 Feb. 2010 <http://findarticles.com/p/articles/mi_m0EIN/is_2008_Sept_3/ai_n28050468/>.

Hagler, E. C. "Improve and Reduce Costs for the Health Care Reform Bill." *Associated Content - associatedcontent.com*. 14 Nov. 2009. Web. 8 Feb. 2010 <http://www.associatedcontent.com/article/2391916/improve_and_reduce_costs_for_the_health.html?cat=5>.

Hake, Tony. "AccuWeather's Joe Bastardi presses case against global warming theory." *Examiner.com*. 11 Sept. 2009. Web. 11 Feb. 2010 <http://www.examiner.com/x-219-Denver-Weather-Examiner~y2009m9d11-AccuWeathers-Joe-Bastardi-presses-case-against-global-warming-theory>.

Hamilton, Tyler. "Can North America's largest coal plant convert to biomass?" *Cleanbreak.ca*. 24 Nov. 2008. Web. 8 Feb. 2010 <http://www.cleanbreak.ca/2008/11/24/can-north-americas-largest-coal-plant-convert-to-biomass/>.

Hareyan, Armen. "Consumer-Driven Health Insurance Replacing Traditional Model, Affordable Health Insurance | *Emaxhealth.com*." EmaxHealth. 27 May 2009. Web. 5 Feb. 2010 <http://www.emaxhealth.com/1/72/31369/ consumer-driven-health-insurance-replacing-traditional-model.html>.

"Health Care." *Department of Veterans Affairs*. Web. 11 Feb. 2010 <http://www1.va.gov/health/>.

"The Health Care System for Veterans: An Interim Report." *Congressional Budget Office*. Web. 11 Feb. 2010 <http://www.cbo.gov/ftpdocs/88xx/doc8892/MainText.3.1.shtml>.

The Heartland Institute. Web. 12 Feb. 2010 <http://www.heartland.org/>.

Hicks, Brian, and Chris Nelder. *Profit from the Peak The End of Oil and the Greatest Investment Event of the Century (Angel Series)*. New York: Wiley, 2008. Print.

Hire A Hero. Web. 12 Feb. 2010 <http://www.hireahero.org/>.

"History of immigration to the United States." *Wikipedia*. Web. 5 Feb. 2010 <http://en.wikipedia.org/wiki/History_of_immigration_to_the_United_States>.

Hoffman, David N. "The Medical Malpractice Insurance Crisis, Again." *www.medscape.com*. 2 May 2005. Web. 8 Feb. 2010 <http://www.medscape.com/viewarticle/503853>.

"How the US Uses Oil." *ProCon.org*. 3 Aug. 2009. Web. 8 Feb. 2010 <http://alternativeenergy.procon.org/viewresource.asp?resourceID=001797>.

"Hubbert Peak Theory." *Wikipedia*. Web. 8 Feb. 2010 <http://en.wikipedia.org/wiki/Hubbert_peak_theory>.

"Hurricane Donna." *Wikipedia*. Web. 11 Feb. 2010 <http://en.wikipedia.org/wiki/Hurricane_Donna>.

"Illegal Immigration and Crime Incidence." *The Federation for American Immigration Reform*. Mar. 2007. Web. 11 Feb. 2010 <http://www.fairus.org/site/PageServer?pagename=research_illegalsandcrime>.

"Illegal Immigration to the United States." *Wikipedia*. Web. 11 Feb. 2010 <http://en.wikipedia.org/wiki/Illegal_immigration_to_the_United_States#Breakdown_by_state>.

"Illegal Immigration to the United States." *Wikipedia*. Web. 5 Feb. 2010
<http://en.wikipedia.org/wiki/Illegal_immigration_to_the_United_States>.

"Illegal Immigration." *www.usimmigrationsupport.org*. Web. 11 Feb. 2010
<http://www.usimmigrationsupport.org/illegal-immigration.html>.

"Immigration Policy Issues." *News Batch*. July 2007. Web. 5 Feb. 2010
<http://newsbatch.com/immigration.htm>.

ImmigrationCounters.com. Web. 5 Feb. 2010 <http://immigrationcounters
.com/>.

Johnson, Hans P. "Illegal Immigration." *Public Policy Institute of California*.
Web. 5 Feb. 2010
<http://www.ppic.org/content/pubs/atissue/AI_406HJAI.pdf>.

"Justice Dept. Figures on Incarcerated Illegals." *NewsMax.com*. 27 Mar. 2006.
Web. 11 Feb. 2010 <http://archive.newsmax.com/archives/ic/
2006/3/27/114208.shtml>.

"K12 for Educators - How Can a Partnership With K12 Help Educators
Serve Their Students? | K12." K12: *Public, Private & Home Schooling
Curriculum - Online High School, Elementary & Home School* | K12. Web.
5 Feb. 2010 <http://www.k12.com/educators/>.

Lance, Jennifer. "From Coal to Biomass: Hawaii to Convert Power Plant."
www.EcoScraps.com. 1 Sept. 2008. Web. 8 Feb. 2010 <http://ecoscraps.com/
2008 09/01/from-coal-to-biomass-hawaii-to-convert-power-plant/>.

Lane, Jim. "US B-1 bomber breaks sound barrier using synfuels as military
steps up on biofuels." *www.biofuelsdigest.com*. 27 May 2008. Web. 8 Feb. 2010
<http://biofuelsdigest.com/blog2/2008/05/27/us-b-1-bomber-breaks-
sound-barrier-using-synfuels>.

Leonhardt, David. "Immigrants and Prison." *www.TheNewYorkTimes.com*.
30 May 2007. Web. 11 Feb. 2010
<http://www.nytimes.com/2007/05/30/business/30leonside.html>.

A Line of Sight. Web. 12 Feb. 2010 <http://www.bobbeauprez.com/>.

Mac Donald, Heather. "The Illegal-Alien Crime Wave." *City Journal.* Web. 5 Feb. 2010 <http://www.city-journal.org/html/14_1_the_illegal_ alien.html>.

Manzo, Kathleen. "Global Competition: U.S. Students vs. International Peers." *Education Week.* 16 June 2009. Web. 5 Feb. 2010 <http://www.edweek .org/dd/articles/2009/06/17/04global.h02.html?qs=global+competition+u.s .+students+vs+international+peers>.

"Marketing Relief for Recession Stressed Entrepreneurs: FAMEE Foundation online marketing course." *www.MissouriBusiness.net.* Feb. 2009. Web. 5 Feb. 2010 <http://www.missouribusiness.net/sbtdc/docs/mktng_relief_recession.asp>.

Mazza, Michael. "Australia Understands the China Threat. Does the U.S.?" *The American.* 8 July 2009. Web. 5 Feb. 2010 <http://www.american.com/ archive/2009/july/australia-understands-the-china-threat-does-the- us/?searchterm=australia%20understands%20the%20china%20threat>.

"Medical Malpractice Tort Reform." *NCSL.org.* 8 Feb. 2007. Web. 8 Feb. 2010 <http://beta.ncsl.org/Default.aspx?TabId=16217>.

Medicare.gov. Web. 11 Feb. 2010 <http://www.medicare.gov/>.

"Mercury - Mercury in Coal." *U.S. Geological Survey Home Page.* Web. 12 Feb. 2010 <http://energy.er.usgs.gov/health_environment/mercury/ mercury_coal.html>.

"Mission and Overview." *U.S. Energy Information Administration.* Web. 11 Feb. 2010 <http://tonto.eia.doe.gov/abouteia/mission_overview.cfm>.

Morrissey, Ed. "Palin: No healthcare reform without tort reform." *Hot Air.* 21 Aug. 2009. Web. 5 Feb. 2010 <http://hotair.com/archives/2009/08/21/ palin-no-health-care-reform-without-tort-reform/>.

Mouawad, Jad, and Julia Werdigier. "Warning on Impact of China and India Oil Demand." *www.TheNewYorkTimes.com.* 7 Nov. 2007. Web. 8 Feb. 2010 <http://www.nytimes.com/2007/11/07/business/07cnd-energy.html>.

Murray, Mark. "NBC poll: Public sours on health reform." *www.FirstRead. msnbc.com.* 16 Dec. 2009. Web. 8 Feb. 2010 <http://firstread.msnbc .msn.com/archive/2009/12/16/2153563.aspx>.

The Nation. Web. 11 Feb. 2010. <http://www.thenation.com/>. *National Archives and Records Administration.* Web. 11 Feb. 2010 <http://www.archives.gov/>.

National Center for Education Statistics. Web. 12 Feb. 2010 <http://nces.ed.gov/>.

The National Committee To Preserve Social Security and Medicare. Web. 11 Feb. 2010 <http://www.ncpssm.org/>.

New Statesman. Web. 11 Feb. 2010 <http://www.newstatesman.com/>.

The New York Times. 3 Nov. 2009. Web. 11 Feb. 2010 <http://www.nytimes.com/>.

Ohlemacher, Stephen. "Number of Immigrants Hits Record 37.5M." *The Washington Post.* 12 Sept. 2007. Web. 11 Feb. 2010 <http://www.washing-tonpost.com/wp-dyn/content/article/2007/09/12/AR2007091200071.html>.

Oliver, Rachel. "All About: Food and fossil fuels." *www.CNN.com International.* 17 Mar. 2008. Web. 12 Feb. 2010 <http://edition.cnn.com/2008/WORLD/asiapcf/03/16/eco.food.miles/>.

Pallarito, Karen. "Fine-Tuning Consumer-Driven Health Plans | work-force.com." *Workforce Management.* Sept. 2007. Web. 5 Feb. 2010 <http://www.workforce.com/section/02/feature/25/11/36/>.

Parker, Randall. "3 Million Illegals Will Enter United States This Year." *ParaPundit.* 13 Sept. 2004. Web. 11 Feb. 2010 <http://www.parapundit.com/archives/002347.html>.

"Peak Oil." *Wikipedia.* Web. 8 Feb. 2010 <http://en.wikipedia.org/wiki/Peak_oil>.

Peron, James. "Ranking the U.S. Health-Care System." *www.TheFreemanonline.org.* Nov. 2007. Web. 8 Feb. 2010 <http://www.the-freemanonline.org/featured/ranking-the-us-health-care-system/>.

Pipes, Sally C. "The Top Ten Myths of American Health Care: A Citizen's Guide." The Heritage Foundation's Lehrman Auditorium, Washington D.C. 12 Mar. 2009. Lecture.

Plautz, Jason. "Health Care Push Revives Tort Reform Debate." *National Journal Online.* 1 Sept. 2009. Web. 5 Feb. 2010 <http://www.nationaljour-nal.com/njonline/no_20090831_5711.php>.

"Popular Ranking Unfairly Misrepresents the U.S. Health Care System." *www.healthandsharing.com*. 1 June 2009. Web. 8 Feb. 2010 <http://www.healthandsharing.com/21/articledetail>.

Raider, James. "Government vs. Capitalism." *Open Salon*. 25 July 2009. Web. 5 Feb. 2010 <http://open.salon.com/blog/pacificgatepost/ 2009/07/25/government_vs_capitalism>.

"Ratification of the Convention on the OECD." *Oecd.org*. Web. 11 Feb. 2010 <http://www.oecd.org/document/58/0,3343,en_2649_201185_1889402_1_ 1_1_1,00.html>.

"Recession could create new generation of entrepreneurs." *www.bytestart.co.uk*. 26 Mar. 2009. Web. 5 Feb. 2010. <http://www.bytestart.co.uk/content/ news/1_12/recession-entrepreneurs.shtml>.

Reidl, Brian. "What Unfunded Mandates?" *The Heritage Foundation - Conservative Policy Research and Analysis*. 3 June 2003. Web. 5 Feb. 2010 <http://www.heritage.org/Research/Budget/BG1663.cfm>.

"Renewable Energy." *Wikipedia*. Web. 8 Feb. 2010 <http://en.wikipedia.org/ wiki/Renewable_energy>.

Roberts, Christian K., and R. J. Barnard. "Effects of exercise and diet on chronic disease." *Journal of Applied Physiology* 98 (2005): 3-30. *Journal of Applied Physiology*. Web. 5 Feb. 2010 <http://jap.physiology.org/cgi/con-tent/short/98/1/3>.

Rothenberg, Stuart, and Nathan L. Gonzales. *The Rothenberg Political Report*. Web. 11 Feb. 2010 <http://rothenbergpoliticalreport.blogspot.com/>.

Rother, John, and Jim Martin. "Issue Clash: Will health care reform help or hurt senior citizens?" *PBS.org*. Web. 8 Feb. 2010 <http://www.pbs.org/ now/shows/health-care-reform/ic-health-care-seniors.html>.

Sack, Kevin, and Robert Pear. "Governors Fear Medicaid Cost in Health Plan." *TheNewYorkTimes.com*. 19 July 2009. Web. 11 Feb. 2010 <http://www.nytimes.com/2009/07/20/health/policy/20health.html>.

Salvi, Steve. "The Original List of Sanctuary Cities." *Ohio Jobs and Justice PAC*. 11 Jan. 2010. Web. 11 Feb. 2010 <http://www.ojjpac.org/sanctuary.asp>.

Savinar, Matt. *Peak Oil, Matt Savinar, Life After the Oil Crash*. Web. 8 Feb. 2010. <http://www.lifeaftertheoilcrash.net/>.

Scott, Thomas. "Tort Reform = Healthcare Reform." *California Citizens Against Lawsuit Abuse*. 10 Sept. 2009. Web. 5 Feb. 2010 <http://www.cala.com/blog/254-tort-reform-healthcare-reform>.

Simcox, David. "Measuring the Fallout." *Center for Immigration Studies*. May 1997. Web. 5 Feb. 2010 <http://www.cis.org/articles/1997/back197.htm>.

Singer, Peter, and Michael Tanner. "Issue Clash: Health Care Reform: Will There Be Rationing?" *PBS.org*. Web. 8 Feb. 2010 <http://www.pbs.org/now/shows/health-care-reform/issue-clash.html>.

Social Science Research Network. Web. 11 Feb. 2010 <http://www.ssrn.com/>.

Squatriglia, Chuck. "Boeing to Test Aviation Biofuels." *www.wired.com*. 21 Dec. 2007. Web. 8 Feb. 2010 <http://www.wired.com/autopia/2007/12/boeing-to-begin/>.

Stang, Alan. "Illegal Alien Crime Statistics." *www.PrisonPlanet.com*. 27 July 2007. Web. 11 Feb. 2010 <http://www.prisonplanet.com/articles/july2007/ 270707Statistics.htm>.

"Sustainable Biofuel." *Wikipedia*. Web. 8 Feb. 2010 <http://en.wikipedia.org/wiki/Sustainable_biofuel>.

Taxpayers for Common Sense. Web. 11 Feb. 2010 <http://www.taxpayer.net/>.

"Teacher Salary Information—United States." World of Education, 12 Dec. 2009. Web. 5 Feb. 2010 <http://www.educationworld.net/salaries_us.html>.

Terrazas, Aaron, and Jeanne Batalova. "Frequently Requested Statistics on Immigrants and Immigration in the United States." *Migration Information Source*. Oct. 2009. Web. 11 Feb. 2010 <http://www.migrationinformation.org/feature/display.cfm?ID=747>.

"A Texas Tale: Carol tells of tort reform." *UnionLeader.com*. 1 Sept. 2009. Web. 5 Feb. 2010 <http://www.unionleader.com/article.aspx?headline=A+Texas+tale:+Carol+tells+of+tort+reform&articleId=c2d6e408-b7af-4b6a-8fb9-ddbbbd88d12e>.

TheLancet.com. Web. 12 Feb. 2010 <http://www.thelancet.com/>.

Thompson, C. M. "Socialism vs. Capitalism: Which is the Moral System." *Ashbrook Center for Public Affairs at Ashland University*. Oct. 1993. Web. 5 Feb. 2010 <http://www.ashbrook.org/publicat/onprin/v1n3/thompson.html>.

"Tips on Dealing with Recession." *Business and Entrepreneurs*. Web. 5 Feb. 2010 <http://www.businessandentrepreneurs.co.uk/tips-dealing-with-recession.html>.

"Tobacco and Cardiovascular Disease." *West Virginia Department of Health & Human Resources Home Page*. Web. 5 Feb. 2010 <http://www.wvdhhr .org/bph/cvd/page1.htm>.

"Trends in International Mathematics and Science Study (TIMSS)— Overview." *National Center for Education Statistics*. Web. 12 Feb. 2010 <http://nces.ed.gov/timss/>.

The United States Army Homepage. Web. 11 Feb. 2010 <http://www.army.mil/>.

United States. Cong. House. Immigration. *Information on Certain Illegal Aliens Arrested in the United States*. By John Hostettler. H. Doc. 9 May 2005. Web. 11 Feb. 2010 <http://www.gao.gov/new.items/d05646r.pdf>.

United States Department of Defense. Web. 11 Feb. 2010 <http://www.defense .gov/>.

United States of America. *Unfunded Mandate Reform Act of 1995*. 22 Mar. 1995. Web. 11 Feb. 2010 <http://sba.gov/advo/laws/unfund.pdf>.

University of Phoenix. Web. 12 Feb. 2010 <http://phoenix.edu>.

U.S. Department of Education. Web. 12 Feb. 2010 <http://www.ed.gov/>.

US News & World Report. Web. 12 Feb. 2010 <http://www.usnews.com/>.

"U.S. Population, 2009: 305 Million and Counting." *US News & World Report*. 31 Dec. 2008. Web. 11 Feb. 2010 <http://www.usnews.com/articles/opinion/2008/12/31/us-population-2009-305-million-and-counting.html>.

Wadhwa, Vivek, Krisztina Holly, Raj Aggarwal, and Alex Salkever. "Anatomy of an Entrepreneur: Family Background and Motivation." *Social Science Research Network*. 7 July 2009. Web. 11 Feb. 2010 <http://papers .ssrn.com/sol3/papers.cfm?abstract_id=1431263>.

Wagner, P. F. *The Dark Side Of Illegal Immigration: Facts, Figures and Data Show A Disturbing Truth*. Web. 5 Feb. 2010 <http://www.usillegalaliens.com/>.

Washingtonpost.com. 21 Aug. 2005. Web. 11 Feb. 2010 <http://www.washingtonpost.com/>.

"Waste to Energy (WTE) & Biomass in California." *California Energy Commission Home Page*. 22 Sept. 2008. Web. 8 Feb. 2010 <http://www.energy.ca.gov/biomass/index.html>.

Welcome to Clark College. Web. 12 Feb. 2010 <http://www.clark.edu/>.

Welcome to Distance Education. Web. 5 Feb. 2010 <http://de.uoregon.edu/>.

Whitman, Christie. "Both sides need to respect debate on health care reform." *www.NewJerseyNewsroom.com*. 4 Sept. 2009. Web. 8 Feb. 2010 <http://www.newjerseynewsroom.com/hot-topic/both-sides-need-to-respect-the-debate-on-health-care-reform>.

Wilgoren, Jodi. "Education Study Finds U.S. Falling Short." *The Rational Radical*. 13 June 2001. Web. 5 Feb. 2010 <http://www.therationalradical.com/documents/teacherssalaries.htm>.

"World Crude Oil Production, 1960-2008." Chart. *U.S. Energy Information Administration*. Web. 8 Feb. 2010. <http://www.eia.doe.gov/aer/txt/ ptb1105.html>.

"Xcel Announces Plans to Convert Electric Plant from Coal to Business." *www.energyonline.com*. 1 Oct. 2008. Web. 8 Feb. 2010 <http://www.energy-online.com/Industry/News.aspx?NewsID=7288&Xcel_Announces_Plan>.

Yates, David. "Poe opposes health care bill, supports Texas tort reform at town hall meeting | Southeast Texas Record." *Southeast Texas Record | Southeast Texas Court News | Litigation—Class Action, Asbestos, Medical Malpractice News*. 13 Aug. 2009. Web. 5 Feb. 2010 <http://www.setexasrecord.com/news/220600-poe-opposes-health-care-bill-supports-texas-tort-reform-at-town-hall-meeting>.